Living in

NORWAY

Photography by Sølvi Dos Santos
Adapted from texts by Elisabeth Holte

Preface by Knut Faldbakken

Flammarion

Design:
Marc Walter
Editorial Direction:
Ghislaine Bavoillot
Typesetting: Octavo Editions
Photoengraving: Colourscan
Maps: Léonie Schlosser
© Flammarion Paris, 199

CONTENTS

NORWAY - ALIVE AND WELL ON THE PERIPHERY

Preface by Knut Faldbakken

Despite its rich and variegated history, Norway has few large-scale historical monuments. Throughout the centuries, this tiny population living on the northernmost fringe of Europe, struggling against geographical and climatic odds that cause visitors from most central regions to blanch, has been more concerned with eking out a living than with erecting monuments to be admired by subsequent generations.

Which is not to say that material hardship and the thwarting effect of long periods of foreign domination on national ambitions succeeded in stifling Norwegians' creative powers. On the contrary, such external pressures seem to have diverted an extremely potent current of creative energy into the many manifestations of folk art. There is a stronger folk art tradition in Norway than in any other European country I know of. And this tradition is revealed both in daily life and in deep-rooted, shared national values in a way not usually associated with a modern nation.

For Norway is, of course, a modern nation—not a living museum. We like to view ourselves as a well-developed, well-run, well-off industrial country. Like our Nordic neighbours, we have created a welfare state on a Social Democratic foundation which has at times served as a model for others. There can be no doubt that we nurture a national ambition to see ourselves as a spearhead of technological, economic and social progress, which is exactly what we are, if the statistics are to be believed.

Nonetheless, few would actually choose to cite Norway as an example of one of the pioneering countries of today's Europe. Our remote location, our difficult topography, our sub-arctic climate and our sparse numbers make us too inaccessible, too exotic for that. And the same applies to our cultural heritage.

Norwegian cultural traditions are not typically European. There is nothing in our history resembling the traditional European city. It is tempting to

attribute this to the fact that there was neither a large enough population nor an adequate material basis for the establishment of large cities in Norway—with one remarkable exception, the city of Bergen, which the German Hanseatic merchants of the thirteenth and fourteenth centuries turned into a flourishing commercial and maritime hub whose tradition-bound, urbane style and ambience still make it unique among Norwegian cities today. At the same time, we must also have to admit that Norwegians scattered throughout our extended, difficult-to-traverse terrain have never shown much inclination to seek each other out in rural communities as in most other European countries. Instead, we have deliberately chosen to settle at a safe distance from all neighbours, though clearly within the shared area that provided a basis for agricultural, forestry, hunting and fishing activities.

In Norway, it is not man-made walls and artificial moats that define a community's perimeter, but the natural boundaries fixed by valleys and mountain ranges, fjords and expanses of forest. The harsh climate has made transport and communications difficult and kept rural districts isolated from one another for long periods of time, forcing each community to rely on its own resources and develop its own local identity. This has given rise to a host of "cultural traditions," each with its own vitality and clearly recognizable local flavour. Instead of stagnating, they incorporated external stimuli in the form of wandering craftsmen such as painters, woodcarvers and cabinet-makers who stopped and worked for a while in the village before moving on, and

in the form of travelling merchants, who brought new textiles, colours, ribbons and the like that were used to renew traditional local costumes.

The political situation also helped to strengthen this thriving cultural tradition on the periphery. Norway was under Danish rule from the beginning of the 1400s until 1814. Our king was Danish, our public officials were Danish, our official language was Danish and our resources and riches flowed into the coffers of the Danish treasury. A Danish-influenced Norwegian upper class did little during this period to preserve the Norwegian national character and identity. But it was, of course, impossible to wholly "Danify" a nation as diversified and spread out as Norway, and the "typically Norwegian" way of life continued to live on in our many villages, hamlets, and valley and fjord communities. Thus, a broad-based, popular national alternative to the Danish-dominated cultural and political elite in Oslo and Copenhagen gradually emerged in the Norwegian outback. And when the nation finally regained its independence, the outlying districts had already firmly established themselves as the taproot of the Norwegian character and the true national values as they had been preserved and developed during the "four-hundred-year-long-night".

This is how there came to be a political and cultural contradiction between city and country which is still alive and well in Norway, influencing many of our values as well as our practical policies. Our capital, Oslo, does not command the same political and cultural dominance in our country as would be expected in a European context. Our outlying districts still view centrally-determined measures and decisions with a certain degree of scepticism, and they know how to use dissent to their advantage. The most powerful pressure groups in politics always have their basis in regional views and the interests of primary industry. The rural parts of Norway remain a rich source of Norwegian talent anchored in local tradition and identity. It is true that the capital acts as a magnet for much of the country's intellectual and creative forces; this is perfectly natural given that the most important political and administrative centres, public bodies, educational institutions and media companies are located here. But it can hardly be said of those who are drawn to the vast opportunities and greater professional challenges of the central regions that they come in the hope of becoming "real" city dwellers. On the contrary, there is a clear trend, perhaps especially among political, cultural or media figures, to preserve their geographical origin visibly and audibly. Remember your roots! Changing one's dialect, tailoring it to the "polished East Norwegian norm" is seldom viewed in a positive light. And on national holidays and similar festive occasions there is no end to the variety of traditional-national costumes to be seen, and which, moreover, are widely accepted as formal attire. The prestige of local culture is sustained up to the very highest level of society.

The question of whether the culture of outlying districts in today's society influences city life as much as city culture influences life on the periphery clearly leaves room for discussion. However, no one would deny that there is a steady exchange in which each side profits from the other, or that this exchange has generated a heated debate, or perhaps more rightly a battle, regarding the path Norway should choose in the face of the new international challenges that have been created by the rapid pace of change in an increasingly integrated Europe. Should we become Europeans, or should we choose to remain the dynamic, but partially isolated periphery we have been for a thousand years.

The answer, of course, must be "yes" on both counts. We can no more turn our backs on the new Europe than we can ignore our own origins and traditions, which embody the foundation of so much of our Norwegian identity.

So while your host in Oslo is likely to appear well-dressed, urbane, sophisticated, well-travelled and linguistically skilled, he may very well invite you to his cottage somewhere rather than to an evening at the opera. And if he – in his own eyes – is truly fortunate, he owns a tiny hut, far off the beaten track, no water or electricity, no neighbours within range of sight or hearing, preferably a half-hour's hike from the closest road, where no signs of encroaching civilization can spoil his view of endless fjords, mountains and sky, cloud his thoughts and introspection, or disturb his longed-for peace of mind and inner harmony. Here in the mountains, by the fjord or deep in the forest, a Norwegian feels at home. Here he can speak of the subtle drama that unfolds as one season flows into another. Here he will find the words to describe changes in wind and weather, the beauty of the flowers, the colours of the western sky, the play of light and shadow, all things that are difficult to define in other languages. Here he can get in touch with the primordial Norwegian dream, the search for harmony in a pact with nature and something essential which has been gleaned from generations of struggle to wrest a living from these same powerful forces. Traces of this quest and dream can be found even in the modern-day Norwegian's most hectic, urbanized existence.

I once took a friend from abroad with me to Lillehammer to show him *Maihaugen*, one of our most beautiful open-air museums of traditional architecture and folk art. He was impressed but somewhat confused:

"I'm not sure I understand what this is supposed to represent," he complained. "If this is peasant art it's fantastic. But if this is the art of the nobility, of the upper class, I must admit I find it a bit primitive…"

I explained to him that the two are not as sharply differentiated in Norway as in the great cultural centres of Europe, and as I did so, I realized that this is exactly what characterizes Norway: there was no dominant bourgeois tradition that took its cues from Europe to become the bearer of a refined, international cultural heritage that repressed the art of the people. Our national traditions have always been too strong for that. The art of the people, our original traditions, have always existed side by side with more sophisticated currents, demanded their due respect and flaunted their quality with a vitality and a self-awareness which is still found today in the countless villages and hamlets tucked away in remote corners of our country.

Still today, these make the Norwegian periphery a nucleus of energy and a source of inspiration in the life of our nation.

Translated from Norwegian
by Carol Eckmann

NORTHERN LIGHTS

With its striking contrasts, Norway is perhaps the most exotic country in Europe. Here, you can go from the cosy intimacy of small painted houses to the unequalled majesty of the natural landscapes: spectacular fjords, islands under the Midnight Sun; idyllic hamlets in vast panoramas; immense forests; silent, trout-filled lakes....

Many Norwegians still wear their luxurious regional folk costume —*bunad*— on all festive occasions. The bunads of Telemark are renowned as the country's most beautiful, with the East Telemark *bunad's* lush, curly embroideries in plant-dyed wool on the black skirt (page 1), and its red, elaborate jacket (page 4). Even the damask apron of the Hallingdal *bunad* (page 2) is richly embroidered. Large farms often had their own precious silver bridal crowns that are still used and passed on from generation to generation. This West Norwegian crown (page 6) is part of the Norsk Folkemuseum's collection. "What imagination could not possibly be amazed to see the Norwegian coasts on a map, with their fantastic jagged outlines and long granite lace where the waves of the North sea incesssantly churn?" wrote Balzac, in *Séraphita*. These coasts are those of the Lofoten islands (page 8), located to the north of the Arctic Circle.

The sea is Norway's jewelry box: the houses are embedded in the mountains and the forests on this Finnmark coast, a region which was the setting for *Babette's Feast*, by the Danish writer Karen Blixen (pages 12-13).

These houses seem miniscule against the impressive Sognefjorden (left) and the lakes of the high plateaus offer tasty catch to fishing buffs (above).

Norway. The word alone evokes images of deep fjords criss-crossed by ferries; the sea's long narrow arms that reflect light deep into the land. Norway evokes mountains and innumerable valleys dotted with charming traditional farms, and deep forest clearings built with hunting lodges and log cabins. Nature, at once immense and familiar, is omnipresent, forming part of the Norwegian reality and the Norwegian imagination; both are enriched by the metamorphoses of the landscape and the lifestyle engendered by the coming of each highly distinctive season. Even Norway's capital, Oslo, is practically part of the countryside—it takes only five minutes to drive from the centre to the wooded hills surrounding the city, or to reach the peninsula surrounded by islands that lies on Oslo's outskirts.

Norway is like a kaleidoscope that presents itself successively and simultaneously under different lights, each transformed by the seasons. Outdoor activities like trout and salmon fishing, deer hunting, sailing or yachting, alternate with a cozy withdrawal into intimate interiors and the domestic pleasures of cooking, weaving, knitting and other crafts. Summer evokes long lazy days along thousands of kilometres of sunny cliffs, silent summers and peaceful islands surrounded by crystal-clear water animated by thousands of dancing reflections called *morild*. Summer brings earthy mountain perfumes, the Midnight Sun beyond the Arctic Circle, and white nights spent gazing at the reddening star floating on the horizon. Autumn summons flaming birch trees and evergreens silhouetted against a pure sky, the first chimney fires, and freshly-aired woollens. Autumn means stocking up on provisions for the long winter to come—berries, game, mushrooms, pickled and smoked fish that reappear in abundance at Christmas time. In winter, the days are so short that it has become a genuine *art de vivre* to stay at home in the comfort of interiors so brightly painted that they seem like childhood dreams. Winter, when friends are invited for a glass of aquavit or a reindeer roast, is a time for dreaming in front of the hearth, or gazing out at the immensity of the night and the moon's blue reflection on the snow. Winter means Christmas—a national holiday—or almost. Spring arrives so suddenly that it makes us giddy; the earth thaws, windows open, flowers pierce the ground, terraces become animated. Spring is so powerful that life suddenly explodes in us as well!

It should hardly come as a surprise that Norwegians who live abroad, or who travel widely, are in unanimous agreement about one thing: they miss life in Norway, nothing can replace it, and they are forever homesick. One could cite innumerable examples of their attachment to their native country: from Ibsen in Rome who longed for the Norwegian sun, to

Liv Ullmann, who preferred, as she explained in her book *Changing*, her desert island Vesterøya on the southern coast near the town of Sande-fjord, to her terrace in California. Describing the particular exoticism of our gigantic little country she wrote, "few places on the earth possess a nature so powerful and so unspoiled that it could remind anyone living in a concrete world that he once belonged to a pre-industrial civilization."

These are sentiments that I understand very well myself, and which are inextricably linked, I believe, to the light, or rather the lights, that transform Norway's islands, coasts, fjords, and mountains into ever-changing panoramas, from Kristiansand in the south, to the Russian border, 1500 kilometres north. This light bestows a sensuality and penetrating spirit on Norway that I carry with me everywhere I travel throughout Europe or America. And it was for this reason that a few years ago, when I left Norway to spend some time in Paris, the French mover who was struggling to carry an enormous farm table up the narrow stairway of my apartment building, said to me, "If you don't mind my saying so, Madame, your furniture is as heavy as lead!" Indeed, with their immediate sensuality, simple forms and bright colours, this glowing wooden table, these artisanal textiles and rustic sideboards preserve the memory of a lifestyle that can be found only in Norway: our way of living among folk art objects that represent the true Norwegian genius, the art of preserving tradition and its ancient rituals in the midst of the most audacious modernity, and of living so

On an autum afternoon on the high plateaus of the country's interior, even the vast châlets seem small (left). These wooden houses are inhabited from Easter until the end of the autumn hunt. In winter, the majority of these houses are only accessible by skis because mountain routes are usually closed after the first snow-fall. The *Nessekongene*, the powerful north coast tra-ding lords, lived on sprawling properties, like here at Kjerringøy (right) on the main coastal shipping lane north of Bodø. The master's house was painted the most expensive colour, white; the shop and service buildings yellow, and those for the fish trade and vis-iting fishermen red. Norwegians love to mix farm antiques with contemporary arts and crafts, such as this vase by renowned glass artist Benny Motzfeldt (below).

close to nature that the country has been described as an ecological model.

Norway's best known personalities—artists, writers, musicians, designers, politicians and industrialists—often have rural roots, and an aesthetic conscience formed through their contact with powerful landscapes comprised of simple, traditional farms painted in vivid colours. That is, unless they are from the seacoasts of the fishermen's cabins so fashionable today, painted red or immaculate white with interiors decorated in primary colours.

Nature has hewn the fiercely indivdualistic character of our people, its art and its adventurous spirit. Munch's Nordic solemnity, his white suns and beaches bloodied by the sunset, seem to exhale the soul of the country he preferred even to the glories of Paris. Ibsen confronted nature with his stifling interior scenes; their penetrating psychological insight and dramatic prose made him a founder of modern European drama. Nature guided the wanderings of Knut Hamsun's memorable characters in a setting of clearly defined, dramatically lit northern landscapes. Nature shaped Grieg's music, where folkloric rhythms dot the more sophisticated accents. Nature is everywhere in architects' love of raw materials—these masters of the art of integrating the habitat into the natural environment; in designer's simple and functional forms; in the sharp outlines and dynamic colours of contemporary painting, whose bold forms harmonize perfectly with interiors that unite the modern and the rustic, wood with metal and thick, hand-woven textiles in natural colours. Nature's influence on generations of explorers who followed the traces of the Vikings as far as North America can hardly be forgotten, nor its power over the famous Kon-Tiki expedition, which received so much attention in the 1950s.

Curiously enough, growing up in this rustic simplicity imbued with tradition, has instilled a strong aesthetic sensibility as well as a solid sense of practicality in the Norwegian people (there are just over 4 million inhabitants in this country which extends more than 1700 kilometres from north to south). The same ecological forerunners now contribute talented artisans and couturiers to the entire world, who are capable of adding a touch of folklore to the most sophisticated urban clothing designs. Two materials are ever-present in Norway: wood and wool, both ancient natural materials, enlivened with the brightest colours found in Europe.

"Authenticity" is the catchword throughout Norway. In this mixture of modernity and tradition there is a force, a sense of national identity, and a concrete feeling of certainty in even the smallest aspects of life— all these are qualities that the outside world resumes rather hastily under the term "Scandinavian." But who are they referring to? The Swedes, the Danes or the Norwegians? It is true that we understand each other's

Heavy, warm clothing is needed during these relentless winters: in a timber-walled hallway, thick, finely-knit mittens wait to be taken out for a walk, next to a fine Laplander hunting knife with a horn sheath (above). In order for these mittens to be useful against the cold and wind, they are first knitted very large, like these on the right, and then washed in boiling water to make them shrink and become as soft and thick as felt. In winter, snow isolates the inhabitants from the most exposed parts of the countryside, as is shown here in the high plains east of Røros (right).

languages and that we are almost cousins, but what a difference there is among us! The Danes, who governed Norway for more than three centuries, live in a magnificent flat country of peninsulas and islands in great conviviality, in love of food and drink.

The difference is less apparent when you cross the immense peninsula on which Norway and Sweden exist side by side, but we quickly realize that there are important differences of style and temperament—the Swedes being generally more urban. We Norwegians form a more distinct people, attached to our rural past, to our country roots—characteristics which are evident not only in the disposition of the people, but also in their style of life—not to mention the pervasive influence of the raw, intense Nature that surrounds us.

Julien Green once compared Norway to Denmark: "In Norway we are in another world, a world wrested from an inflexible nature by a

The *Ivistoga* hall (right) at Yli farm in Telemark is one of Norway's finest folk art interiors, with 1797-1807 richly carved box beds and exquisite rose-painting. The lush, colourful rose-painting, *rosemaling*, by renowned local masters, involved far more than mere flower decorations and usually did not include any roses at all. In many valley's dialects, *rosut* (rosy) simply meant decorated; rose-painting was the general name for the luxuriant rural decorative art in the 18th and 19th centuries. At Holm farm (above) in Os in North Østerdalen, a fireside folding table was a favourite place for reading in winter. In the old days, weaving cotton rag rugs (left) was a way to make use of worn household textiles and clothes.

people that has never known fear. Norway is the land of great contrasts." Describing the inhabitants of the banks of the steep-walled fjords he added, "They live at the base of this fantastic wall in their small painted houses. . . . They seem so calm in this setting that would present a challenge to the most audacious visionaries." Yet Green could carry this contrast further: "This landscape makes us want to stay here forever. With its meadows crossed by brooks, its hills and orchards, it is the ideal setting for a kind of happiness that has become so rare today."

The respective architectures of the three Scandanavian countries are eloquent in this respect. As far back as ancient times, the Swedes usually constructed lightweight buildings with wooden facades, while the Danes, who claim practically no forests, built their thatched cottages in stone and clay; the Norwegians built their solid valley farms of logs, one farm often made up of twenty buildings for different uses.

Norway is a truly ancient nation whose independence is relatively recent. The first kingdom was founded in the late 9th century by King Harald Hårfagre. Then Norway came under Danish domination. The Danish king sided with France in the Napoleonic Wars, and Norway was then ceded to Sweden when Napoleon was defeated in 1814. But the Norwegians rebelled, and on 17 May 1814 they adopted a constitution for a free, independent and democratically governed Norway, giving rise to the growth of national identity. It was only in 1905 that Norway became a monarchy again with the coronation of the Danish prince Charles (the grandfather of the present King Harald), who came to the throne under the name Haakon VII. A renewed national consciousness was expressed in architecture and furnishings by the adoption of the Dragon style, inspired by a pseudo-Viking nationalism.

As a people, therefore, we are both old and young, which explains the dominant rural trait in Norwegian culture. An independent spirit has resulted from it—the farmer is master of his domain isolated in the middle of his lands often far from the sight of his closest neighbour. In the evening, when travelling in the countryside we glimpse the glowing windows of these scattered farms, and only then do we understand the scarcity of the population of this countryside, a place to which city dwellers dream of escaping at the slightest occasion.

Now it only remains for you to discover our country, which is at once heroic, by the amplitude of its natural setting, and intimate, through the warmth of its interiors. Nothing is as important as outdoor life and the comfort of home; it is as if the dichotomy between outside and inside constitute the very structure of daily life. The passage between them has resulted in one of the world's most unique lifestyles.

Norwegians usually prefer antique farm furniture to their urban counterparts. Mr William Jensen, who inherited several pieces of fine farm furniture, has spent a lifetime collecting even more. The kilim-cushioned bedside "sofa" in the bedroom (right) of his Oslo apartment is an especially fine 1824 box bed, like those found on farms all over southern Norway in the old days, often built along with the farmhouse itself. When winter's snows rule outside, homemade apple pie in a spacious Oslo apartment kitchen (below) substantially raises morale.

WINTER

Christmas by the fireside: in the intimacy of richly
decorated rose-painted Telemark farms,
on high plateaus in small timber houses with beautiful
rustic furniture, and in Dragon-style villas
on Oslo fjord. A traditional Christmas by the light of
sparkling candles that illuminate the long night.

These white woollen gloves were worn by the bride and groom in winter but also by church-goers (preceding pages). Found all over Norway, these ravishing open air museums of traditional art have preserved the old houses with turf rooftops which otherwise would not have withstood the assaults of "progress". The most important of these museums are the superb Norsk Folksmuseum of Oslo and that of Maihaugen in Lillehammer (left) where one of the small dark farms lays buried in the snow, among the birch trees said to be "as gracious as young girls", by Balzac in *La Comédie Humaine*. A sled used for transporting logs is waiting in front of the fence. At the first snowfall, Norwegians unpack their *sparkstottinger* (above), an ingenious sled created in the 1920's: this is an ecological transportation method that, propelled by foot, often replaces the automobile.

The snow is back! Across Norway's mountains, forests, open fields and ragged coastline, the days are growing shorter and the nights longer—and colder. In the immense darkness, lighted windows look like small gleaming eyes. On innumerable wooden porches, skis stand ready for the trails and slopes after work or on weekends. The whiteness creaks under your boots, the frozen breeze tickles your face and your breath condenses before you, forming steam clouds in the air.

Fireplaces light up in city flats, suburban houses and farms. Big, woollen handknits and puffy, comforting eiderdowns are taken out of closets. When friends drop in, hot spicy wines are served. As winter draws in, Norwegians fortify themselves against the encroaching cold and dark with food. Indeed, after a reindeer roast, a steaming pot of lamb in cabbage or some smoked, cured meats, always accompanied by beer and aquavit, morale is so high that you cannot imagine life without the arduous, sensuous, cocooning experience of a Norwegian winter.

Ask a Norwegian abroad what he or she misses most about Norway and the answer will almost certainly be winter. Powerful images of the winter landscape are engraved on the Norwegian psyche: the sharp outline of bare branches or the jagged silhouette of cliffs against the endless cover of snow; the miles upon miles of forest filled with living Christmas trees; the low winter sun and the freezing fog wrapping itself around the fjords and islands on the west coast.

Winters in Norway are particularly long and intense. A midwinter day can be as many as thirteen hours shorter than a summer day. For people living in the mountainous areas, the season has already begun by late September and it lasts until April or early May. For others, the snow does not arrive until after Christmas and has gone again well before Easter. In the northern town of Tromsø, the sun disappears completely for fifty-four days in winter. The only natural light comes from the northern lights, made by nature's own electrically-charged particles flashing in the pitch darkness like giant laser beams.

Despite the severe weather and the prolonged darkness, or perhaps because of them, winter draws together and cheers this nation of strong-willed individualists. Human warmth is indispensable for facing up to the fierce winter snowstorms. When winter is at its darkest, Norwegians throw themselves into the family feast of light—Christmas.

A FARM CHRISTMAS IN VESTFOLD. "For us," says Ingegerd Mender, looking out at the spacious courtyard in front of her elegant, white-panelled, 18th-century house at Studsrød farm, "Christmas means candles and fireplaces, family cooking traditions, and the annual scrubbing of whitewashed pine floors with soft green soap." For Mr and Mrs Mender and their children, Christmas also means spruce trees decorated with lights—indoors and outdoors—candlesticks decorated with red apples, and the family's traditional blue and white Danish china which is taken out of the antique, painted sideboard of the spacious, low-ceilinged dining room where it is usually kept.

The farm, which the Menders bought some years ago, is situated west of Oslofjorden, Oslo's fjord, at the end of a forest road in Vestfold county. Oslo, where Per Georg Mender spends his working week as a lawyer, lies ninety minutes away by bumpy country track and main road. The Studsrød farmhouse is now the family's year round home, and the perfect setting for a rural Norwegian Christmas. The intimate, elegant, little rooms have white-beamed ceilings and crackling fires, cast-iron ovens and stylishly curtainless, 18th-century windows with deep candlelit bays. Poinsettias, with their striking scarlet bracts, nuts, colourful apples, and freshly polished brass candlesticks are scattered amongst Norwegian and Swedish town and country antiques. The Menders' *kilims* may not be Norwegian, but they are close enough in spirit and design to Norway's own traditional woollen tapestries to harmonize with the rest of the decor.

At Studsrød farm, the traditional Christmas meal consists of a huge succulent rib of pork with sour cabbage, followed by cloudberries in whipped cream, and accompanied, of course, by beer and aquavit. Some families here in the east of the country prefer a mouth-watering ham with cloves, but although the Christmas dish may vary from home to home, aquavit and beer, are a constant. No Christmas or winter meal of heavy pork or lyed fish is complete without the potato-based, caraway-spiced spirit to put a sting to it. It is best to drink the *akevitt*, or *dram*, straight from the icebox, when it is so cold that the bottle whitens with frost. As the only spirit produced in Norway, *akevitt* is the country's national alcoholic beverage. It can be brownish in colour or clear. Norwegians prefer the brownish version which has been aged for at least a couple of years to give it a rounder, gentler, spicy taste. This is what you should drink with dry, cured meats or the heavy pork dishes. Clear aquavit, aged for less time, has a more distinctly caraway and anise spiciness which best accompanies heavy fishes such as lyed cod, marinated salmon or pickled herring. Aquavit is drunk out of a tiny glass, and custom demands that it be downed in one go. Once you have drunk it this way you will realize why it is always served with a generous glass of beer—the beer is needed to put out the fire!

At Christmas, farm interiors across Norway glow in the candlelight, like here at 18th-century Studsrød in the forests and fields of Vestfold county, west of the Oslo fjord. The dining room's antique farm cupboard with engraved wooden doors (right), comes from neighbouring Numedal valley and was decorated in 1804 by acclaimed local folk art painter, Kjetil Haukjem. In the old days, this cupboard was used to store food but today it holds the family's fine Royal Copenhagen china. The chairs are Norwegian Hepplewhite from the early 19th century.

In the kitchen, Mrs Mender has prepared Christmas Eve's succulent pork ribs (above) with all the trimmings.

The cool refinement of the Studsrød farmhouse is accentuated by the main living room's curtainless windows (above), lining a gilt 18th-century Swedish mirror above a light Gustavian sofa, also from Sweden, Mrs. Mender's mother's native country. Decorating the spruce Christmas tree is a family affair, as are baking and other preparations before the kitchen is scrubbed and decorated for Christmas Eve (left) and its chandelier hung with heart-shaped pepper biscuits. But according to a national tradition that is more practical than religious, all the Christmas frills must be gone by *Trettendagsjul* (the thirteenth day after Christmas or Holy Three King's Day, on January 6th).

Norway's Christmas menus vary enormously from region to region. In the west of the country, *pinnekjøtt*, or steamed, salted ribs of mutton, with potatoes and mashed turnip, is a favourite. In the southern coastal area known as the Sørlandet, and in the coastal regions in the north, boiled cod is preferred, unless you observe the *lutefisk* tradition, and marinate dried cod in a potash lye in your basement for several weeks. On Christmas Eve, many families across Norway, both in the country and in towns, observe the tradition of a quick lunch of *risengrynsgørt*, a rice porridge with an almond hidden inside it. The person who finds the almond is entitled to a small extra gift. The Mender family, like all Norwegians whatever their Christmas Eve tradition, awaken on Christmas Day to an enormous buffet lunch, which includes various kinds of marinated herring, cold or smoked meats, cold racks of rib, and bulging white pork sausages.

The Menders and their guests are not the only ones to benefit from the farm's lavish Christmas rituals. On Christmas Eve, among the haystacks and the collection of antique sleighs in the barn, the family leaves a pot of the traditional rice porridge for Nissen, the Christmas gnome, or for Santa Claus himself, with his red stocking cap. The horses, the family's riding companions throughout the year, get an extra serving of oats, while the birds who did not migrate south for the winter descend on the sheafs of corn. On the thirteenth day after Christmas, the trees and all the decorations have to go, even though Christmas actually lasts until Easter, if an old Norwegian song is to be believed.

THE DRAGON STYLE. Wherever you live in Norway, you are always close to nature. From the centre of Oslo, you are just a few minutes by car or tram from vast expanses of evergreen forest, with downhill slopes, miles and miles of ski trails, many of which start out from the famous Hollmenkollen ski jump, and numerous hospitable lodges. On sunny winter weekends, the lodges in Nordmarka and the neighbouring pine- and spruce-filled areas look like colourful ant hills, teeming with daytripping skiers from all walks of society. Sitting in one of the elegant, rustic, turn-of-the-century timber Dragon restaurants high up in the hills, you can take in the magnificent view of Oslo and its fjord dotted with innumerable little islands.

The Dragon, or Viking style was officially reviled for decades, but has recently come back into favour. This nationalistic Nordic style included furniture, silverware, and architecture, and numbers of striking Dragon villas are to be found all over Norway. With the revival of interest, inherited Dragon chairs that had been banished to the attic are now being brought down for a fresh look. The style originated in Sweden at the beginning of the 19th century and spread to Norway. The Swedes and the Danes tired of it in the 1880s but Norwegians maintained the Dragon style and used it as a symbol of their ongoing struggle to leave the threadbare union with Sweden, which ended in 1905. Considered a pure Scandinavian tradition, totally independent of what was happening on the continent, the Dragon style was an expression of the pride of the Viking age. In the 1880s and 1890s, many Dragon hotels, railway stations, sanatoriums and villas were built throughout the country.

Some of the Dragon buildings have burnt down, but among the most striking examples which remain are the Frognerseteren Restaurant, where many people go for warm apple pie in winter, and the

The Ekheim villa on the outskirts of Friederikstad, designed by the architect Ole Sverre between 1896 and 1900, has all of the rich symbolism of the Dragon style, in both its interior and exterior decoration. Friederikstad was named the 'planktown' and was famous for its sawmills located on the Glomma, a river which transported wood from the Østerdalen valley all the way to the north. When industrialized sawmills developed in the middle of the 17th century, houses constructed in logs gradually made way for houses built with wood planks and painted in vivid colors. The red and white façade of Ekheim is an example of this. Upon entering, we are welcomed by stylized dragons (left). The dining room (right) is a remarkable testament to the national pride which took over the country in 1905 after its separation from Sweden. The monumental mahogany furniture from Cuba (1898) and the brass Viking chandelier were also created by Ole Sverre who decorated the buffet with motifs of the same style (above).

Set on a forest-covered hill, the 1894 Dragon style Holmenkollen Park Hotel towers above Oslo (left). Its elegant, rustic, timber-walled restaurant *De fem stuer* (the five rooms) (right) offers a buffet lunch with every possible type of succulent, marinated or smoked salmon and pickled herrings (below), followed by typical Norwegian salted or cured meat. A large, strongly national romantic painting which harmonizes with the building itself is Gerhard Munthe's well-known 1890 depiction of a farm in the rich Hallingdal valley. The restaurant also owns a painting by Theodor Kittelsen, the famed 1857-1914 painter beloved by Norwegians of all ages for his illustrations of the fairytales, collected in the 19th century, that became an important part of Norway's literary heritage.

Holmenkollen Park Hotel and Restaurant, situated high on the hills above Oslo. The latter has been expanded today and is probably the capital's most sensually beautiful place for a winter lunch. In charge of its kitchen is young Bent Stiansen, one of Norway's leading chefs, who represents his country at the gastronomic world championships in France. His rosette of wild smoked salmon from the fjords of western Norway, accompanied by a lemon mousseline and followed by a filet of reindeer from Trysil in the east, along with forest mushrooms, rounded off with a mousse of cloudberries from the north, will fortify you against the coldest winter day.

Another dramatic example of Dragon architecture, but with a warmer atmosphere, is the huge red and white wooden villa, Ekheim, owned by Hroar Hansen and his wife, Mrs Bitten Bekkevold Hansen, located near the seaside town of Fredrikstad, close to the Swedish border in the south. On winter weekends the Hansens and their friends retreat to this welcoming old villa. When they acquired the place, more or less everything had been left as it was at the turn of the century. Recently the villa has been completely restored with heavy dados and the original wallpapers in the interior; old woollen tapestries decorate the walls. The living room walls are of round timber and are covered with hunting rifles. Romantic images of Viking ships dominate Ekheim's furniture and lamps, providing a striking contrast with Mr Hansen's high-tech professional activities in electronics and publishing.

THE HEART OF OSLO. With every passing day during the period leading up to the *vintersolverv*, the winter solstice, on the 21st or 22nd December, the daylight hours become shorter. Then, to everyone's relief, the day finally turns, as they say in Norway. For practical purposes, there are only two or three hours of daylight at this time of year and people tend to remain indoors. Even in the south, midwinter days are so short that by the time Oslo workers go home for dinner at around 4pm, it is completely dark. To cheer themselves up on the way home, some Osloers stop for a plate of steaming boiled cod or lyed fish at the intimate Engebret Cafe, Oslo's oldest restaurant, dating from the 1850s. It is an informal place, set in a low-ceilinged little house built in the 1760s. Opposite is the sculpture courtyard of the Museum of Contemporary Art, which is housed in the huge, old, fortress-like Central Bank building. The Engebret's Cafe has always been a hang-out for people working in the arts and media. It is situated in the old part of Oslo, in what is left of Christiania, the town built by the Danish-Norwegian King, Christian IV, in the early 17th century. The old city is now being renovated and turned into Oslo's most attractive cultural area, with flourishing museums and galleries.

Another place for heart- and body-warming gastronomy is the monumental, high-ceilinged Theatercafeen, the Hotel Continental's 1901 Viennese brasserie. The Theatercafeen is one of the most popular places to eat in Oslo and is particularly renowned for its reindeer *rôti*. It has tall, rounded windows which provide a perfect view of street life outside, dark wooden wall benches and large mirrors. In the afternoon, people are entertained by a pianist who sits high up in the little orchestra balcony. The walls are covered with drawings of the major cultural figures from the country's past, some of whom more or less installed themselves permanently at the Theatercafeen. The place still attracts writers and painters, as well as lawyers and business people. Some of the customers prefer to sit at the tables among the pillars, from where they can keep a close watch on who comes and who goes, and with whom. Others set up camp on the more discreet wallside benches. Anyone wanting to get a real feel for Oslo life should head straight for the Theatercafeen. The place is like a lifestyle stock exchange—with all kinds of stocks and all kinds of exchanges, depending on the time of day.

When you have finished your meal at the Theatercafeen, you can go and watch the moon as it lights up the quiet harbour waters around the Aker Brygge, or pier, Oslo's new, vibrant area of flats, offices and restaurants. From the waterfront, you can see Akershus castle rising proudly above the piers on the opposite side of the harbour. Many of

In the new neighbourhood of museums and art galleries in the centre of Oslo, the old restaurant Engebret (above) is admired for its steamed *lutefisk* (lyed fish), eaten just before Christmas with beer or aquavit. A few streets away, the Theatercafeen (right), the Viennese café in the Hotel Continental, has been the favourite meeting place for the artistic and business media crowd for generations. In winter, the lights of the packed café, which is just across from the National Theater, shine across the street. Oslo's city center, where restaurants used to close early a few years ago, is now lively until late at night.

The oldest of the ten delightful timber farm houses that Mr Martin Mehren has collected on Oslo's hill is a 14th-century hearth house. The 1799 farmhouse from Hjartdal in Telemark county is a particular jewel with its magnificent box bed and adjoining dressers, (left) along with the lovely shelf stacked with wooden plates (following pages) constructed, according to the tradition, as an integral part of the house. In Mr Mehren's 18th-century Valdres valley house, there is a fine rural clock from Biri, near lake Mjøsa (top), and old wooden farm tools leaned up against an elaborately carved storehouse door (above).

the flats are furnished with huge, elegant, old farmhouse tables and other country antiques, in sharp contrast to the functional brick and cement construction of the buildings.

The most sought after apartments in Oslo today are the large old flats in the mainly residential areas behind the Royal Palace. However, other, generally well-off people prefer to live just outside the city, on the surrounding hills. In the past, these vast hills were used as summer pastures for Oslo's farms, but around the turn of the century, a large timber hotel, a few villas and a sanatorium were built there so that people could benefit from the fresh air. Over the last two or three generations, spacious homes have been constructed here that take advantage of the commanding views of the city and fjord below. Beyond the hills lie *blåne på blåne*, mountain range after mountain range, extending for such a distance that the furthest ranges are just a bluish shimmer on the horizon, recalling the evocative pictures that used to illustrate old Norwegian fairy tales.

FROM ARCTIC EXPLOITS TO ANTIQUES. Some of the houses on the hills around Oslo were moved from their original locations in the valleys by enthusiasts for old timber farm architecture. In this way, whole villages have been created on these gently sloping forest-covered hills, where every little grass-roofed house serves a purpose. Martin Mehren and his sons are veteran timber home owners. Today, the Mehrens are retail magnates, but fifty years ago, Mr Mehren crossed Greenland on skis, and in 1990 his son Herman reached the South Pole as part of an all-Norwegian expedition sent to emulate the achievement of their compatriot Roald Amundsen, who led the first successful expedition to the pole on 14th December 1911.

After Mr Mehren created his 'farm' of small attractively weather-beaten farmhouses, his sons Preben and Herman, who followed their father into business, also followed his example of collecting folk art and renovating old timber buildings. The houses have low doorways, and traditional, spacious, all-purpose rooms filled with antique farm furniture, often of huge dimensions. The peaceful, pastoral home life enjoyed by the Mehrens up in the hills seems far removed from their businesses in Oslo's city centre below.

Many Norwegians have fallen for the charms of old wood, whitewashed wooden floors and finely rose-painted or stencilled walls, tables and bowls. Most Norwegian houses outside the densely populated city centres are made of wood. This is partly because much of Norway is covered in forests, but also because the culture is rooted in rural life.

The typical village, town, or suburban home is a small, two-storey family house on a quarter of an acre of land filled with roses in summer and covered with snow in winter.

For two or three generations, there has been a craze for antique farm furniture and objects in Norway's towns, ranging from fine and costly 18th-century tables and dressers to a more basic lyed farm table or antique wooden bowl. It is only recently that urban antiques have started to attract attention. Many of these come from Sweden, Denmark and Norway's southern coast, and are made from birch or old English mahogany in the Empire style. However, *bondemøbler*, or old farm furniture, remains the most sought after type of antique. Some Oslo antique dealers specialize in it—Kaare Berntsen's, Olav Skrindo's, Gard's and many other similar shops are like small folk art museums. The appeal of this furniture grows as it ages: the old painted wood, sensuously worn at the edges, is so smooth that its refined colours shine out. These luminous antique pieces are highly desirable, but highly expensive as well.

Even in the most modern Norwegian homes, it is unusual not to find at least one small remnant of the country's rural heritage—a bowl, a table, a rose-painted chest of drawers, or a painted dresser. (It would also be unusual not to find an example of Norway's innovative contemporary handblown glass or pottery.) Up until the middle of this century, there was little appreciation of antique farm furniture in the rural areas and much of it was bought up cheaply by city dwellers and dealers. These days, most farmers value their heirlooms—their painted beds, massive tables and rose-painted or stencilled walls—and take good care of them. On some farms, whole interiors can be works of art, because craftsmen not only made furniture but also carved and painted entire rooms, including the bonded timber walls and the ceilings. Baroque tendrils and rococo shells adorn the massive wooden walls and beamed ceilings, while carvings of soldiers or kings with sabres drawn, bring doors to life. Many of these 18th-century rooms still survive intact in farmhouses in the valleys and on the lowlands of southern and eastern Norway. Some are still used by the descendants of their original owners. Often, though, the present-day owners have built themselves modern houses next to the old ones, with 'luxuries' such as electricity and plumbing.

Norway's rose-painters are, in their way, as distinguished as any of the country's more widely known cultural representatives. But rose-painting was a rustic art made by local masters who travelled from farm to farm, often spending months in one place carving and painting

the most magnificent interiors. The tradition of rose-painting started at the beginning of the 18th century and reached a peak towards the beginning of the 19th, surviving until the middle of the 19th century in some regions. For the owners of the houses, rose-painting was a way of expressing new-found prosperity, and farmers and peasants wanted to show off their wealth and their improved social status, much as the prosperous merchants and civil servants in the towns displayed theirs.

A rich and complex folk art, rose-painting was an amalgam of local tradition and personal style. Artists generally knew of the major artistic trends and skilfully incorporated this knowledge into their designs. Although rose-painting lagged behind stylistically in relation to the major artistic trends that were evolving on the continent, you can nonetheless find elements drawn from all the major styles—Renaissance, baroque, rococo and Empire. The leitmotif of rose-painting, the elegant, sweeping baroque tendril, could play different roles within a design, in conjunction with flowers, in elaborate geometric patterns or as a structure for other motifs. Popular motifs included human figures (the artist might paint the farmer's wife if he found her pretty enough), flowers, trees, religious scenes, and soldiers on horseback with little dogs running at their feet. Artists chose pure, bright hues to produce vivid but harmonious effects.

Because each artist had his own style and because local traditions were so strong, it is easy to identify the part of Norway from which a particular painted chest or dresser comes. The region of Telemark and the Hallingdalen, Numedal and Østerdalen valleys are among the areas that have produced the finest rose-painting. A number of artists in these regions achieved notoriety at the end of the 18th and beginning of the 19th centuries. Aslak Nestestog and Olav Hansson, Hans Glittenberg, Knut Mevasstaul, Thomas Luraas and Talleiv Maalar were prominent exponents of the Telemark tradition.

A number of rose-painters were also skilled fiddlers, because the two traditions often went hand in hand. Thomas Luraas was from a family of renowned rose-painters and fiddlers and seems to have been quite a character. Together with his brothers, he set up a painting school. He was pursued by the authorities for counterfeiting, and is said to have paid for his board and lodging on farms by decorating rooms with his ornate paintings. One of the most renowned 18th-century painters in the lowlands to the east was Peder Aadnes. He created delicate, baroque, floral designs in soft blues, but his style tended to be more 'urban' than that of his fellow masters. When rose-painted furniture attributed to Peder Aadnes or his fellow masters appears on the

Until the 18th century, only church interiors had rich, colourful interior decorations. When the rose-painting tradition began to enter people's homes, religious scenes were among the favourites. But angels, like those on this Norsk Folkemuseum 1806 chest (right) from a farm in the Hallingdal valley, were rare. From around 1800, the free flowing flower and rocaille rose-painting in the North Østerdalen valley became more symmetrical, with flowers arranged in urns or garlands. The masters of this new tradition included Ole Andersen Beitdokken, who painted the intimate rooms of Holm farm in Os in 1833 (above). Legendary rose-painter Thomas Luraas, as famous for his young, wild counterfeiter days as his exquisite rose-painting, decorated this magnificent double box bed (preceding pages) surmounted by a richly decorated cupboard that Mr Erlend Grostad of Flatdal acquired from a neighboring valley farm some decades ago.

Norway's history will forever be linked to its strong polar traditions and such great names as Fridtjof Nansen, Roald Amundsen and Otto Sverdrup. In the tower of the Polhøgda villa, home of renowned polar explorer, philanthropist, diplomat and 1922 Nobel Peace Prize winner Mr Nansen, the office (left) remains exactly as he left it before his death on May 13th 1930. Papers include letters (above) regarding the "Nansen passports", internationally recognized identity certificates that he made for World War I refugees stranded with neither identity papers nor travel rights. Mr Nansen's efforts on behalf of Russians saved between 1.5 and 2 million refugees, particularly from the Volga and Ukraine, from dying of starvation.

antique dealer's circuit in Norway today, you have to be prepared to pay enormous sums for a major item such as a sideboard. However, the colours and forms are so beautiful that you could put that sideboard in an empty room and need little else.

Rose-painted rooms are still used on special occasions, such as family reunions during holidays. At such times, the enormous, colourful built-in beds are pressed into service and the iron stoves lit. Although old timber houses may look picturesque and the decoration may be sumptuous, you often need to wear thick sweaters - sometimes even in bed - when winter really begins to bite in January and February.

A**N EXPLORER'S BASE.** A number of Norway's most prominent personalities have chosen to make their year-round homes in the seclusion of the forest-covered hills around Oslo, where they are within easy reach of the centre of the city. The dark brown villa called Brattalid (steep hill), on the slopes a short way below the Mehrens' property, belongs to Norway's grand old polar couple, author and explorer Helge Ingstad and his archaeologist wife, Anne Stine Ingstad. The couple's discovery of an archaeological site at L'Anse aux Meadows in Newfoundland provided crucial evidence to prove Mr Ingstad's theory that the Vikings had arrived in America five hundred years before Columbus set sail in 1492. This creative and determined professional partnership between Helge, born two days before the new century, and Anne Stine has been rewarded with doctorates the world over, as well as membership in London's prestigious Royal Geographical Society. Helge Ingstad has been a lawyer, a trapper, and governor of Spitzbergen Island and Norway's province in north-east Greenland. Now in his nineties, he continues to write about Viking history in close collaboration with his wife.

It would be hard to envisage a more appropriate setting for the Ingstads than Brattalid. Built amid the trees and set behind wooden gates, it was named after the Greenland farm of Erik Raude, the Norwegian-born discoverer who was exiled to Iceland in the late 19th century. Under the high timber ceiling, a carved head looks down from above a window, while Mr and Mrs Ingstad's fine collection of old knives competes for attention with a variety of interesting urban antiques.

For years, Mr Ingstad has had an office in the large villa called Polhøgda, or polar height, which used to be the home of polar explorer, refugee, administrator, humanitarian and Nobel Peace Prize winner Fridtjof Nansen. Polhøgda is located on the lush green peninsula west of Oslo and is now a bustling institute for arctic research. Nansen's office in the tower, which commands a superb view of the fjord,

The best of European urban and Norwegian rural styles meet in the living room (right) of explorers Anne Stine and Helge Ingstad's dark wooden villa on the forest-covered hills above Oslo. The English mahogany Empire furniture is a family heirloom, and the blue farmhouse door is attributed to Peder Aadnes, the late 18th-century rose-painter from the flatlands around Mjøsa lake who combined rural and urban elements in his art. Mrs Ingstad bought the rural rococo chair from a Lillehammer antique dealer. Her father was legal adviser to Nobel prize-winning author Sigrid Undset, and she had admired such chairs in the author's home. Mr Ingstad bought the elaborate *sendingskurv* (above, traditional food basket of *teger*, the longest and most elastic birch roots), in the Numedal valley as an engagement present for his wife in 1941.

has been left just as it was before his death in 1930. It still contains his old typewriter and dictaphone, as well as letters and other souvenirs.

Down by the water is the Fram Museum, named after the majestic *Fram*, the ship on which Nansen embarked for his expedition to the North Pole in 1893. Nansen failed to reach the Pole, but he got closer than anyone before him. For the next 20 years, the Fram served other prominent polar explorers. Captain Otto Sverdrup used it on his expeditions to Arctic North America, followed by Roald Amundsen for his historic expedition in 1910, when he conquered the South Pole.

A DESIGNER'S HOME STAGE. When it comes to farm antiques, William Jensen, Oslo fashion and theatre set designer, has more than most in his loft on the quiet residential Riddervold Street, behind Oslo's Royal Palace. "I have quite a lot of space, and I was born during the war, so I never throw anything anyway. And the fact that I am a collecting maniac and have been stage-struck all my life, makes my flat a curious *mixtum compositum*" says Mr Jensen, with a mischievous smile. In the summer, home for Mr Jensen is a simple seaside cabin on a nearby peninsula. His city centre flat, however, provides a warm and welcoming setting for the inventive winter meals he cooks for his friends.

Mr Jensen's parents had refined tastes and owned many antiques. In the 1930s, they were among the first to decorate their city dining room with farm furniture. The first antiques he bought himself were a lyed writing desk and a small dresser chosen as part of a revolt against what he regards as the horrors of the early 1950s. Since then, he has not stopped. His Norwegian and Continental collection contains many items of painted antique farm furniture including voluminous canopied farm beds, sideboards, tables and chairs, and he even has a lush blue Peder Aadnes sideboard in the sitting room. In addition to antique furniture, he has amassed a multitude of small, charming objects, selected with a designer's eye for form, and arranged to create surprising colour combinations and playful effects.

OLD FARM BUILDINGS IN LILLEHAMMER. The area around Lillehammer is particularly rich in old dark or white timber farm buildings and antique furniture. Lillehammer, site of the 1994 Winter Olympics, lies a couple of hours drive north of Oslo, where the wide Gudbrandsdalen Valley slides into the Mjøsa, Norway's largest lake. One of the most striking properties in the area is the 17th- and 18th-century Lysgaard farm, owned by Sidsel and Arve Skaarseth. Like a number of farms in the region, the buildings at Skaarseth are clad in white panelling. Its

When Mr William Jensen seats his dinner guests around the Renaissance table (above) in his spacious town centre apartment, some sit on the baroque German church bench. This bench, with its carved angels' heads, once stood in Stavanger Cathedral. But Mr Jensen and his friends generally take their candlelit meals under the beams in the kitchen (right) which is furnished with an old farm table and unmatched chairs, while the winter winds roar outside.

thirty-metre-wide main facade is embellished with carved brown window frames and doors.

The past is present everywhere at Skaarseth. The property has been in Mrs. Sidsel Skaarseth's family, the Bergsengs, for many years and she ensures that the numerous rooms are kept beautifully furnished with the mahogany and birch pieces that had been so popular in the early 19th century with the rural leisure class. The family silver is here, along with paintings from Norway's Golden Age of the end of the 19th century. Lysgaard's greatest indoor treasure, however, is its canvas wallpaper dating from the 1750s. Birds and fruits, flowers, landscapes and houses are painted in refined, vivid colours still surprisingly fresh. Absent for many years from the walls at Lysgaard, the wallpaper had been rolled up and stored away from the middle of the 19th century until it was rediscovered in 1920.

A LAKESIDE FAMILY HOUSE. Just south of Lillehammer, the red and grey buildings of Svennes farm spread out across the fertile flatlands by the banks of Mjøsa lake. "When we moved from the city and took over Svennes, which was completely empty of furniture at the time, we wanted to make the farm a home for a modern family, with all the modern facilities. Then we started to move a panel here and a panel there, and gradually we fell in love with the place. It became a passion, a lifestyle, and a lifelong adventure to recover the original soul and spirit of the place," explains Margrethe Sand. Over a period of fifteen years, she and her doctor husband, Anton Bratberg Sand, have painstakingly restored this huge manor, the home of Mr Sand's ancestors, the founding fathers of Norway's 1814 constitution. Standing on the banks of the frozen lake in winter, Svennes, with its huge grey main building and red barn with its clock tower, is the very picture of an aristocratic Norwegian farm.

To say that Svennes provides spacious accommodation for the Sands and their three daughters would be an understatement. The main house offers 1000 square metres of living space and the two upstairs ballrooms can seat one hundred people. There are forty-seven buildings in all for the Sands to maintain on their two family farms, Bratberg and Svennes. The family uses their entire house, except for the two ballrooms, all year round, and can choose among a succession of sitting rooms, each with its towering fireplace, antiques and old panelling, to spend their winter evenings. The kitchen is furnished with a large farm table, two old fireplaces—one which provides light for working or reading by and the other for cooking in—and an iron stove in the centre for heating.

The old photo-album (below) illustrates the powerful family traditions that reign on the large aristocratic Lysgaard farm in Lillehammer. This house, built on a hillside near the olympic village, has living-rooms furnished in Empire and other ancient styles, and is decorated with beautiful examples of Norwegian landscape painting. The lovely cast-iron pot is an antique; it was made in 1776 in the Baerums Verk studios, on the outskirts of Oslo. The house is especially proud of its richly-coloured wallpaper (right). Such wallpaper was rare and could only be found in the country's wealthiest residences. The silk cushions are the work of generations of Lysgaard women.

"Svennes is a house you have to commit yourself to," explains Mrs Sand, a dark-haired, attractive woman who is known throughout the country from her job as television presenter in the early 1970s. "Many years ago, when I was studying philology at Oslo University, I wanted to be an architect, to study the history of art and learn the arts and crafts. Here at Svennes I have been able to do it all!" she laughs. "It is absolutely fascinating to live in a landscape that changes so much with the seasons. You have the clean, white expanses of winter followed by the black, freshly ploughed fields in spring, which a few weeks later have turned light green. Then summer arrives with its lavish and colourful abundance, followed by the fertility of autumn, before the fields once again turn white with snow."

The restoration of the main house at Svennes with its thirty-five rooms and seventy-two windows, was not an easy task for the Sand family, who took it over in 1974. The main building alone consists of six separate houses that have been gradually merged in an extended building process over several centuries, with styles ranging from 17th-century baroque at one end of the house to turn-of-the-century Swiss at the other. In between, one finds rococo and Empire elements. The Sands admit that you have to love old houses to live in a place like Svennes because there is no end to the work that needs to be done to keep the property going. Doctor Sand, who shuttles between hospitals in Lillehammer to the north and Gjøvik to the south, plans Svennes'

Approaching prosperous Svennes farm (left) by way of the wide, flat fields along lake Mjøsa's frozen shores, you arrive first at the red barn buildings of this large property that once belonged to one of the founders of Norway's 1814 constitution. The hospitable family that now owns the farm have forty-seven large and small buildings to take care of. In the seventy-square-metre kitchen, there are two fireplaces; the white, round one (right) was a *lyspeis*, a fireplace to give light to people working beside it. The *teger* basket contains *flatbrød*, the flat, crispy bread eaten with cured and smoked meats (below).

farming and forestry activities and administers the 150 acres of agricultural land and 2.500 acres of forest himself.

The family's goal was not to make everything perfect, but to let the house vibrate with life again. They enlisted the help of conscientious national experts and Mrs Sand has spent hundreds of hours working on the house, as well as acting as a live-in arts historian. In room after room you find original windows with handblown glass. The woodwork has been lovingly restored and repainted, using such traditional Norwegian painting techniques as marbling and stencilling. Much patient experimentation was needed to produce a finish with the right glow.

Svennes is a hospitable farm, especially at Christmas when there is plenty of room for guests and plenty of good food as well. The Sands take full advantage of each season's particular possibilities, for each season has its own crops and its own domestic rituals, like washing and starching all the curtains. After her husband's hunting trips, Mrs Sand fills the farm's cooling room and huge freezers with meat, makes elk sausages, collects wild mushrooms and prepares all sorts of mouthwatering dishes from pork, to lamb, ox and elk. Herring from the lake and fermented trout are favourites for the family's traditional Christmas party which is the occasion for innumerable varieties of cakes and biscuits as well. The original baking oven, located in one of the sitting rooms, is still used for breadmaking and Svennes' name is burnt into the loaves with the old kitchen iron.

ARTS AND CRAFTS IN TELEMARK. One of the regions in which the folk traditions of Norway are most vigorous is the hilly, forest-filled

Even in winter, the Sands' heat and use most of the one thousand square metres of Svennes' main building (left), but the two huge upstairs ballrooms are closed off during the cold months. In the glowing yellow *Bondestuen* (Farmers' room) (right), the family serves fermented trout at their traditional pre-Christmas party around the old Cook's table, which was named for the two fold-out wooden beds beneath it, where kitchen maids slept, two to a bed, in the old days.

county of Telemark, west of the Oslofjorden. Handicrafts such as woodcarving, silver jewelry-making and knitting live on here. Each region has its own national costume, or *bunad*. Women of east and west Telemark don these costumes for festivities rather than a party dress, even in the cities. For unlike other national costumes, Norwegian costumes are still regularly worn on special occasions and those of east and west Telemark, with their rich embroideries and silver jewelry, are widely regarded as the most beautiful in Norway.

One of the most interesting interiors in Telemark can be found at Yli farm. Yli, with its white main house and red barn, is situated on snowy slopes near the community of Heddal, not far from the industrial community of Notodden, whose factories provide employment for many people who live on farms too small to provide a proper living. The delightful and colourful hall on the second floor of Yli, added to the main building in 1797, is famous. Its elaborate canopied beds were made by carpenter Niri Madsen in a Renaissance style and painted by Olav Hansson in 1807, and are among the finest examples of Norwegian folk art. Yli contains other pieces of fine furniture—dressers, beds, and a writing desk, or *skatoll*, built as an extension to a bed—all painted in an emphatic Renaissance style. A mounted hussar, one of the Telemark painters' favourite motifs, is depicted on the door. And as religion was central to life in those days, Olaf Hansson added an inscription to the canopy of the beds which he painted in such beauty: "True fear of God is the seed of all good virtues. It leads us to what God and the Law command us." Above the long, massive farm table at Yli hangs something which, in this proudly traditional and strongly rural interior, is a surprising fragment of the Continental heritage—an antique Venetian mirror.

At Yli, family life has been marked by generations of hardworking and fastidious men and women. The fine linen was spun and woven by the now deceased grandmother, Tone Yli, and it features plant-coloured *krullar*, traditional folk-art curled motifs. The family's old textile heirlooms are meticulously preserved by Mrs Yli, who has a strong interest in and knowledge of traditional woollen tapestries and embroideries. How does Mrs Yli keep the wonderful paintwork from peeling and the untreated wooden floor clean? "Just wash with soft soap water and then let it dry," she explains. Nor is she a stranger to other traditional household techniques. One of these involves lying dried stockfish bought on the coast, first by putting it in water for four days, then in lye for four days, and then back in water for a further four days. It will then be ready to serve at Christmas as *lutefisk*, or lyed fish, alongside the traditional pork meat dishes.

In his *Norwegian Rose Painting*, rose-painter and researcher Nils Ellingsgard describes how economic growth in Norway in the beginning of the 18th century brought considerable changes to the farms. Fireplaces and iron ovens replaced open hearths, and more and more windows were added. The furniture remained an integral part of the building itself but became more elaborate. The first pieces of sophisticated furniture, after the beds, were the armoires, dressers and corner buffets, and later, hanging cupboards and grandfather clocks. Rose-painting gradually became more elaborate and luxurious, as the upstairs hall on Yli farm in Heddal (above and right) illustrates. This superb farmhouse interior was carved by local carpenter Niri Madsen in 1797 and decorated by famous rosepainting artist Olav Hansson ten years later.

A FARM IN THE HEART OF SKIING COUNTRY. Telemark is renowned for its skiing as well as its folk art, and not just because the traditional Telemarking technique, which has become popular at ski resorts around the world, was born here. According to winter sport legend, Telemark is where skiing itself originated. Within Telemark, Morgedal, an area where scattered farms nestle among rolling, wooded hills and fast-flowing rivers, could claim to be the cradle of skiing. It is the home of ski pioneer Sondre Norheim, and has been fittingly chosen as the city where the Olympic flame will be lit for the winter games in Lillehammer in 1994. In Morgedal, skiing is not just a pastime for visitors who come to stay either in their *hytte*, or holiday cabins, or in local hotels—it is a way of life for the local inhabitants.

In a forest clearing in Morgedal, up a steep, narrow dirt road which turns off the main road linking east Norway with west, lies Donstad farm. This old family property is an amalgam of some fourteen separate houses that farmer and businessman Arvid Gjersund and his wife, Laila, have taken over and made their home. The couple also owns the old fashioned general store on the main road. The oldest of the Donstad timber houses date back to the early 17th century, but most were built in the 18th and 19th centuries. These houses have been rebuilt and restored through the years, in cooperation with the authorities responsible for national monuments, and the result is an exceptionally fine Telemark farm. The main outbuilding shelters the animals and farm equipment; the *iøe*, or storehouse, is for the hay; the *treskelåve* building is for the grain thrashing tools, a henhouse, a *stabbur*—the traditional food storehouse built on pillars to prevent mice from getting in, which was used in the past for stocking salted, dried food in winter—a woodshed, a sauna, a forge, and a stone firehouse. Further on, there is an outbuilding for the summer pastures.

Today, the Gjersunds and their children lead their contemporary lives in the listed main house, keeping strong ties with life as it was lived in the past. Donstad's main house has not always stood where it stands now. Part of it dates back to 1609 when it was a one-storey building. It was moved here in the late 18th or early 19th century, and the family became sufficiently prosperous to add the *ivistoga*, or upstairs room, making it the two-storey building it is today. The owners wanted their new *ivistoga* to be a grand festive location for the family's great occasions. So in 1850, they had the renowned Telemark artist Knut Olson Mevasstaul decorate it in the style of the day. The doors and beds are beautifully painted in green, pink, white, orange-reds and blues; delicate cloud motifs decorate the ceiling. It is no wonder that

On the *Donstad* farm, situated in a clearing of the Morgedal valley region of Telemark, the end of a built-in bed had been embellished by purely functional elements: a grandfather clock and a pottery shelf have been added next to a convenient folding table (left). The main house, which dates from the beginning of the 17th century, has many more of these roomy built-in beds, mostly in the *Ivistoga* (Upper Hall), the farm's finest, decorated by rose-painting master Knut Olson Mevasstaul in 1850. Across the snow-covered yard (above), the striking little 19th-century red *bur* or *stabbur* (pillared storehouse) stores dried, smoked hams and other meats throughout the winter. Donstad also has a similar, two-floor loft; the extra floor was used to store precious objects and to lodge guests. Snowy Morgedal was the home of Sondre Norheim (1825-97), who broke with 400 years of skiing traditions by inventing bindings fixed around the heels.

Donstad's *ivistoga* is regarded as one of the finest in Telemark. Everyday life was led downstairs, but whenever important guests came to visit or there were family occasions to celebrate, the upstairs stove was lit and the *ivistoga* opened up.

Downstairs the fine furniture—a built-in bed and an old fireside table—is less elaborately decorated. What attracts the attention, however, are the bare pine floors with their strange square inlays of various dimensions. The inlays conceal a simple but ingenious method for sorting potatoes. In the past, when the potatoes had been harvested, they were brought into the living room and moved around on the floor until they found the hole of the right size and fell down, sorted, into the right part of the cellar. The rooms at Donstad are small and multi-purpose. Today, the Gjersunds have only four children, but there were thirteen in the previous generation. Having so many children helped you to keep warm in the winter.

Although the next-door neighbour lives a mile away, Donstad remains as friendly now as it was in the past, when a visitor would always be served a cup of coffee and a glass of dram. These days tourists often walk past the farm to have a look at this charming little private village. Since this is hunting country, game figures prominently on Mrs Gjersund's party menus, particularly at Christmas, as do trout and perch, fished from the Morgedal lake before it freezes over. At Christmas, people from farms around the region gather in the little white church a few miles away, just as they gather at the big local cattle show in September. In Telemark, there are rituals that nobody wants to miss.

THE PRIVATE WORLD OF A WOODCARVER. Sveinung Svalastoga was a painter, poet, and woodcarver who created a strange fairytale world on a farm in Rauland, a ski resort area in Telemark, on the edge of the Hardangervidda mountain plateau. Here, by the shores of a vast lake, transformed into an expanse of dazzling whiteness in winter, picturesque farms are scattered among the fields and sparse trees. Svalastoga is the area's oldest farm; part of the main house and the *stabbur* date back to the 15th century. It is now owned by Sveinung Svalastoga's heirs who use it as their holiday home. Sveinung Svalastoga cut and carved his mystical figures from the twisted mountain pines, until his death in the late 1950s. The figures of a sensuous woman and her man guard the entrance to the main house whose porch is decorated with old millstones, while a pensive fairy-tale princess keeps a watch on the corner of the *stabbur*.

Donstad farm's little *ildhus* or blacksmith's forge (right), made of wood like the other buildings, stood at the far end of the square courtyard. The fear of fire was great in a country where most houses have been made of wood since the Viking days, and where many fine old buildings have gone up in flames over the centuries. Doors of old farm outbuildings are often a symbol of non-ostentatious refinement (below).

The winter feels less biting here in this inland region than on the coast. When the days turn longer and the sun becomes insistent, the snow seems to glisten with diamonds, your face tans, and Svalastoga's timber buildings, with their grass roofs, start to warm up.

Woodcarving is still an important part of life in Telemark and the region is renowned for its beautifully carved knives. These ornamental knives are favourite gifts for men on important occasions, from confirmation onwards. In Notodden, the knife-maker Mr Olav H. Wåle has a four-year waiting list for his knives with their exquisitely worked hardwood handles.

LIVING IN THE PAST. When you drive into Rauland from the east, you immediately notice the Lognvik family's property, Austbø (the eastern farm). The farm stands high on the hillside of fields. It consists of twenty-five timber farm buildings grouped around the main house, Nystog (the new house), built in the late 18th and early 19th centuries. The fine upstairs room, which is called an *yvistova* in Rauland, is a living folk art museum, and is one of Norway's most famous, best preserved folk art interiors. The colourful blue or red built-in beds, the dresser, the walls, and the ceiling were all elaborately painted in 1841 by local artist Hans Glittenberg who had already painted the downstairs some years earlier.

If Austbø farm stands high on the hillside today, its location was considerably less prominent until the late 18th century, when the farmer moved his buildings further up the hill for more sun and better views. Not all of the buildings that make up the farm today were part of the move, however. The oldest buildings date back to the 14th and 16th centuries, others to the late 18th and early 19th centuries, while the most recent were built in the middle of this century. Austbø is a farm on which many generations have left their stamp.

These days, the *yvistova* is used for big family reunions, including birthdays, weddings, and baptisms. When Mr Lognvik and his wife Tone lived in Nystog, before their large, modern wooden house had been built, their newborn baby would sleep between them in the big bed in the *yvistoga*. With temperatures outside falling as low as -25 to -30° C, it was so cold even indoors that the baby had to wear a woollen cap in bed. During the coldest days of the year, the steep staircases cannot be washed for the steps would quickly freeze. The big fireplace and cast iron oven provide some heat, but somebody has to get up first in the mornings to light the logs. Only then does a little warmth start to permeate the house.

In the rich folk art areas of Telemark, twisted tree trunks appealed to creative minds, like that of artist Sveinung Svalastoga, who, at the beginning of the 20th century, decorated the exterior of his Svalastoga farmhouse (above) in Telemark county with woodcarvings and millstones.

Olav H. Wåle of Notodden continues the fine knife-smith tradition; his handmade knives have shining handles of *valbjørk* (right), a birch that is particularly strong and veined by the bark growing into the wood.

The Lognviks like to follow the strong local traditions. At Christmas, they have fish soup and steamed trout from nearby rivers, with *kling*—the local flat, soft bread—a sweet homemade beer, smoked legs of lamb, sausages and various other good meats which have been hanging appetisingly in the *stabbur*. The older people in areas like Rauland still know the old recipes, and continue to use them. The younger generation, who have jobs in the oil business, schools and broadcasting alongside their farm activities, increasingly buy their food in local shops. On national holidays, however, everybody upholds the traditional practices. Keeping one foot in modern professional life, and the other in traditional farm activities is a demanding business—besides working in the oil industry and mass communications, Mr Lognvik cuts the forty acres of hay that he uses to feed hundreds of sheep through the winter months.

In the old days, additional floors were often added to single-floor buildings when the farm prospered, and famous local rose-painter Hans Glittenberg was commissioned to decorate the new room on the top floor (*yvistova*) (left and right). He had already richly painted the oldest room (above and top) along with its built-in beds, and dresser. To this day, the Longnvik's receive guests in the *yvistova*.

The colourful, elaborate exterior of Oddentunet farm (left), now a museum, is quite a work of art in this region of heavy snows south of the legendary old mining town of Røros. In the middle of Røros itself, Mr Amund Spangen, of the North Østerdalen Museum Authority, lives in the 1796 house once belonging to the old manager of the town's provisions. In his small, low-ceilinged kitchen he mixes lamps of contemporary Danish design with a farm table and Budal armchairs (right). Making these simple, functional wooden chairs gave the farmers of Budal valley, northwest of Røros, some welcome extra income during the winter months. Old and modern kitchen accessories are right on hand (below) in Mr Spangen's home.

A LEGENDARY MOUNTAIN MINING TOWN. Nowhere are Norway's cold winters colder than at Røros, a mining village on the high mountain plateau south-east of Trondheim, the historic seat of Norwegian kings from the early 13th century up until the beginning of the Danish reign in 1380. At Røros, temperatures of -40° C do not raise an eyebrow and the harsh conditions have formed people with a rough sense of humour. Nowhere else does the snow creak quite like this under your boots or does your nose get so red under your sheepskin hat, and nowhere else can you see your breath so clearly in the air. In winter, the villagers tend to use alternative means of transport for getting around, and there are more *sparkstøttinger*—sleighs that you kick forward standing up—than cars. Røros and the neigbouring village of Os stand at the far end of the huge forest areas of the Østerdalen, the eastern valley. When travelling through this long, flat-bottomed and forest-covered valley, you frequently see elks emerging majestically from the trees to cross the road.

Copper has been mined on the mountain plateau since the 18th century, and has brought prosperity and international trade links to the region. Røros, one of Norway's finest architectural villages, has been classified by UNESCO. The two main streets are lined with low, brightly-painted houses dating from the 17th, 18th and 19th centuries. The town's famous black and white wooden church is a prominent landmark in the middle of the immense, flat, highland landscape.

At Røros, knitting, carving, and bark wickerwork traditions live on. The southern Laplanders are also a strong presence here. The town and its history have gradually taken on a semi-mythic status in Norwegian culture through the epic novels of Johan Falkberget, set in the mining community. The sagas of his heroine An-Magritt have become part of the literary heritage of all Norwegians.

Amund Spangen has made his home in the 1796 timber-panelled Proviantskrivergården (the house belonging to the clerk of the town's provisions) in Røros' main street. Mr Spangen's residence befits a man who works for the North Østerdalen Museum Authority. In the intimate rooms between the thick, round timber walls, he has amassed a wonderful collection of old furniture and objects, all of which have a story to tell. Some of them belonged to his own family, others came from friends.

"The important thing with furniture and bits and pieces that you surround yourself with, is that you should know something about them," says Mr Spangen. And he has a wide repertoire of entertaining tales about the old expandable sliding beds, the massive chests, and the laplanders' knives with horn handles. When he moved in, the restoration work was in progress, but he made it clear that he did not want any of the quirky angles straightened or the marks that past generations had put on the house covered up, preferring to live among the visible traces of things that had happened there before his time.

Life moves along at its own pace in Røros, and Mr Spangen adores living here. The people are particularly open and friendly, and they come and go in each other's homes freely, although things did go too far one day, when Mr Spangen went out into his courtyard to get some firewood and returned to find complete strangers walking around his living room. They were tourists who thought that his home was one of the town's mining community museums!

Some of the prosperous old farms in the area are no longer in family hands, but have been turned over to museums so that they can be enjoyed by everyone. The late 18th-century Oddentunet farm on the riverside just south of Røros is one of three such particularly delightful old farms. The elegant two-storey main building shows how prosperous the Røros mine made the inhabitants of Oddentunet. The exterior displays yellow panelling and bright, elaborate, shuttered windows and the pink and golden interior is richly adorned with delicate stencilling, lush flower paintings, marbling, and carvings. The original owners, Mr Rasmus Knudsen and his wife Anne, had their home decorated in 1822—the year was traditionally recorded on the wall as part of the design.

Oddentunet provided its owners with a spacious 200 square metres

The sumptuous pink interiors of Oddentunet farm, richly decorated by local rose-painters in the early 19th century with symmetrical floral arrangements in neat baskets, was inhabited until 1968 but retains an opulent atmosphere. In 1822 and 1826, Oddentunet's rich owners, who had stock in the Røros mines, had their interiors decorated with horns-of-plenty over a built-in bed and the cradle beside it (above). A finely carved and painted decoration over the door (right) indicates that you are entering the house's finest room, with its grandfather clock in black and gold china design, flower garlands above the windows and on the elegant little beams. The finely worked farmchair backs attest to the wealth of the estate.

The listed 1779 Holm farm sits on the highland plateau near Røros. Traditional blue marbling on the door frame (left) adds a touch of refinement to an unusually strongly-coloured interior. One of the huge furs in which people wrapped themselves for winter sleigh rides hangs in the hallway. The cellar (top) was used for stocking potatoes through in the winter, while the *stabbur* above it held meats and other food reserves that would later end up on wooden plates in the farm kitchen (above).

of luxury accommodation, with one sitting room for everyday use and one for special occasions. The built-in bed with its painted cornucopia on the wall, the charming little wooden cradle beside it and the neat 1807 cupboard above, give you a real sense of how the people of that era lived. Across the snow-covered courtyard stand the twin timber storehouses, the *stabbur*, which held the salted and dried foods that fed the family and the farm hands through the long winter. Forming the third side of the yard and offering additional quarters is a stylishly unpainted and weather-beaten grey timber building with a striking, panelled yellow entrance.

Delightful as it is, however, Oddentunet is not an easy house to live in by modern standards. So, after its thorough renovation, the Odden family—Mrs Marit Odden and her son, Knut Sigvart Odden, and his family—have retreated to the comfort of their contemporary farm a few yards away, leaving the charms of old Oddentunet to the Os municipality as a museum. From time to time, Mrs Odden makes her way past the metal and wood fence that separates her present home from her old one, to show her cherished Oddentunet buildings to visitors who may also be fortunate enough to taste some of her special creamy waffles. The old Oddentunet tradition for hospitality lingers on.

THE YELLOWS OF ØSTERDALEN. John Holm Lillegjelten has held onto his family's old Holm farm in Os, a few minutes out of Røros. The farm, with its fine 1779 main house panelled in the strong, reddish yellow characteristic of North Østerdalen, is a conspicuous presence in the midst of winter's gleaming white mountain plain and bare trees. The Østerdalen forestry valley is one of the richest regions for Norwegian folk art. During the 18th and 19th centuries, some farms amassed discreet fortunes thanks to their enormous forest properties, although fortunes fluctuated with the good times and the bad times of the forestry business. At Os, up on the high flatlands, the trees are frail, but with income from Røros' mines and trade in the 18th century, Mr Lillegjelten's farmer ancestor Knut Baarson and his wife Maret commissioned their house with its severe, refined exterior.

Holm's main building, listed since the 1930s, is an architectural gem. The two large living rooms, one on either side of the small timbered entrance hall display elegant, stencilled paintwork. The steep, narrow stairs lead to two bedrooms. Mr and Mrs Baarson's prosperous son, John Knudsen and his wife Anne Lisbet, further enriched the house, and it was they who, in 1833, commissioned the local painter Bedokken to decorate the living-room walls in the same North Østerdalen yellow.

The large main room of Holm farm (right) along with the adjoining small bedrooms and baby cradle were painted the rich ocre yellow so often seen both inside and outside the wooden houses in the open landscapes of North Østerdalen. The Holm farm walls were painted in 1833 by master painter Beitdokken whose Louis XVI inspired floral decorations began a new, stylized rose-painting tradition. The tall white grandfather clock was made by local artisan Amund Bøe, from neighbouring Røros. The 1855 iron stove was indispensable for the inhabitants of this house who endured freezing cold winters here until 1918. The sword on the farm's lush ocre wall (above), between the decorated doors leading to the kitchen and the entrance hall, belonged to a relative who lost his fortune when he left the farm to fight against the Swedes in 1719.

The paintwork displays refined stencilling, lush flower festoons, urns, and family inscriptions. The tall, built-in grandfather clock, decorated in white with gold, was made by local master Amund Jacobson Bøe at Røros. An iron stove with a charming fold-down flap was installed to add to the heat from the open hearth in the corner.

Today, Mr Holm, like many other owners of old houses, has moved into a more modern building on the property. But he remains the custodian of the family treasures, including his ancestors' enormous sleigh fur coats with soft, red, woollen linings, which hang in the beautifully simple 18th-century hall ready for the next ride.

A NORWEGIAN'S *HYTTE* IS HIS CASTLE. Whether you live on an old farm in the country, or in a town, winter is a way of life in Norway. Even when spring comes, many Norwegians cannot let winter go, and during the Easter holiday week, they rush to the mountains to catch the last of the snow. Consciences or bosses permitting, they stay for up to ten days of ski and sun. Old soldiers never die and neither do ski-loving Norwegians for whom their *hytte*—their holiday cabin in the mountains—is their castle.

Hyttes are often simple log cabins, but they are highly sought after at Easter, when temperatures creep up from the -20°C in midwinter, and the sun guarantees a striking tan to take you into spring. The typical skier at this time of year might be a young Oslo media professional who wants a quiet break skiing in the mountain air. He will probably drive the four hours up from Oslo to the family villa at the top of the Hallingdal valley, one of Norway's best skiing areas. His villa will have a commanding view over miles and miles of ragged mountain plateau, a view he can enjoy from the comfort of the glazed veranda. The interior offers him a cheerful retreat with round timber walls painted bright blue, red or yellow, fireplaces with continuously burning fires and comfortable, stylishly rustic furniture and old woven textiles.

After Easter's last glorious days of skiing in the mountains, the skiers return home. The year pulls irresistably on towards spring, and life in Norway, both indoors and outdoors, suddenly goes into a different gear.

AN ARCHITECT'S HOUSE. Mr Jørn Narud's house stands on a quiet road lined with villas in Oslo's West End. In the summer, half hidden and softened by tree foliage, the dark brown, two-storey house could be mistaken for hundreds of other wooden shoeboxes around Norway. But in winter, when garden and house stand out with graphic clarity, you can fully appreciate what a unique home Sally Jane and Jørn

The views are impressive from this spacious 1915 mountain villa's sun-drenched glass veranda (right), hung with an antique *akle* (Norwegian tapestry), overlooking the Hallingdal valley (right) from the top of mountain plateaus. The villa's four living rooms built with round timber walls (below) are filled with casually elegant antiques and hunting and fishing mementos. A Turkish *kilim* covering a sofa and traditional Norwegian tapestries on the walls bring East and West together here.

The Narud house in Oslo (top) was awarded a prize in 1990 for its use of concrete as a building material, in striking contrast to the tarred wood of the old 1928-29 functionalist part of the house. The upward movement of the design makes the tall house on the top of the low hill seem even taller and more striking. Contemporary Oslo artist Øyvind Svaboe's lively painting (left) and an amphora (above) found in Aix-en-Provence provide additional decoration for the downstairs entrance hall.

Narud have created for themselves. Turning the corner at the top of the little garden path, you are struck with the contrast between the inconspicuous, traditional wooden house and the new concrete addition. What looks from one side like a tarred, panelled 1950s house, becomes a striking example of modern architecture on the other.

Mr Jørn Narud, an established architect, designed the addition so that the dramatic contrast would be invisible to the neighbours—everything happens on the garden side away from the road. The Naruds have created a warm, clean-lined home by combining naked concrete, glass, and bright primary colours, with contemporary furniture and striking modern paintings, like Ulf Valde Jensen's bold canvas above the dining table. A lot can happen behind discreet Norwegian wood!

AN ECOLOGICAL LIFESTYLE. For generations, the picturesque, hilly island of Nesøya to the west of Oslo was owned by the Blehr family. The island is now linked to the mainland by a bridge, the formerly secluded bays are filled with pleasure boats, and the slopes have progressively been covered by post-war Norwegian architecture of an adventurous kind. The island is far from built up, though, and if you drive through the courtyard of the old main farm, you find yourself on a small forest road that seems to lead nowhere. But then, on the top of an open slope among the trees, you suddenly encounter journalist Karin Blehr's loft house, built on 125 acres of listed volcanic land by a lake full of pike and perch. Many rare and old trees still survive, as do rare flowers, in this remnant of the primeval European forest which has disappeared everywhere else but here and in Poland.

What Mrs Blehr values most about this location is the freedom to lead a self-sufficient, ecological life. She can, if she chooses to do so, live off the land by hunting and fishing—a great privilege when you are so close to the country's capital. The property is extensive and the house, which was designed by Mrs Blehr herself over a period of years, is correspondingly spacious, with seven metres under the steep eaves. Everything in the house remains subordinate to this dramatic space, with its unusual perspectives, and light, open mezzanine. Apart from the kitchen, bathroom and bedroom—with a snow-level window through which to watch the foxes, hares and badgers from the bed—the whole house is one big room.

Mrs Blehr has lived and worked here for two years and describes the house as "raw, avant-garde and tolerably refined." The generous interior, with its tree trunk pillars and contemporary steel and wooden furniture, blends modern design and American frontier style. Works by

Roy Lichtenstein and Andy Warhol, and paintings by her artist husband Bjørn Ransve hang on the walls. In the centre of the room a towering fireplace, inspired by the 13th-century Norwegian farmhouse hearth tradition, stands next to an ecology-friendly woodburning stove; together they ensure that the house remains warm in the coldest winter.

A writer on art, Mrs Blehr sees her house as a kind of self-portrait. For her, a house is just as much a personal statement as the jewelry and clothes people wear. Her statement combines the traditional Norwegian hearth-house and a modern use of space in a room where she can live out both her professional and her private lives on her own hidden patch of snow-covered primeval forest.

Mrs Karin Blehr built her new home on the family grounds of Nesøya island near Oslo, and the result is a striking loft house (left and right), whose huge living room is seven metres high. "Inside and outside co-exist," she says. When you approach the house on a late winter night, the high, tent-shaped window on the top of the open slopes reveals the large open space within. The Indian painting by her artist husband Bjørn Ransve, whose studio is in a separate house, underscores a rustic atmosphere created by the barked tree trunk pillars. The central stone fireplace (above) and woodburning oven beside it heat the whole house in winter, adding to the pioneer spirit.

SPRING

Spring makes its first appearance on the banks
of the magnificent western fjords where rococo
and Empire homes open their doors and windows wide
to greet the new season. Music lovers
crowd into Grieg's villa and onto Bergen's piers.

Suddenly, spring arrives. After months of endless snow cover and cocooning darkness, it feels as though a huge door has been flung open in our lives. Across the country, freshly cleaned windows are opened, and crisp ironed curtains waft in the gentle breeze on old timber balconies. Plump eiderdowns are aired after the long winter, and blonde wooden floors are scrubbed fresh. In the gardens, brightly coloured tulips and crocuses appear, unfolding and stretching towards the sun while fruit trees are transformed into clouds of white or pink flowers.

The familiar, insistent sounds of spring fill the air—melting snow drips from the eaves of steep, red tile roofs and bloated rivers roar. To the west, where spring arrives first, streams of glacier water add a dash of green to the fjords and rambling old hotels fling open their balcony doors to welcome the new season. Birds returning from Africa and the continent join those that stayed behind in impromptu choirs on the beaches and in the forests. Branches of birch trees that were nothing more than stark lines etched against the snow, abruptly unfold veils of intense, fresh greenery. Fields that until recently had been expanses of snow become black, steaming tracts of earth behind the farmer's plough before suddenly turning green. Plump little anemones peep upwards at the feet of forest pine trees where just a short time ago you rushed by on skis. Children gather the blue anemones and yellow coltsfeet to decorate kitchen tables.

Even the most hardened urban cynics will admit that the newly opened birch leaves, the bursting pussy willows, and the ever lengthening days are a tremendous tonic after the long winter. All along the coast, people are readying their small boats for the outdoor season. And even if most of the old wooden craft of our childhood have been abandoned in favour of fibreglass boats, this remains an important spring ritual. Others concentrate on their gardens, attending to the roses that survived winter's ravages, planting new flowers and preparing the vegetable garden.

In Oslo, the less energetic head for the café terraces which have been set up for the season's first beers, by the park on Karl Johan Street, between the ochre brick buildings of the national theatre and the parliament building. Some opt for Aker Brygge, Oslo's newest urban development overlooking the harbour in front of the massive, twin-towered red-brick city hall. Others, chiefly members of Oslo's artistic community, prefer the Vigeland sculpture park whose outdoor terraces have been described as the 'summer pastures' of the Theatercafeen.

Outdoor life explodes throughout the country and all along the coast, even though April weather is notoriously unreliable and can turn

Glaciers like this one, the Josterdalsbreen (right), which is the largest in Europe, dominate the blossoming hamlets with their imposing crystalline, blue-tinted mass. Spring's first flowers create a path among the barren rocks (above). *Mangletrër* (long pieces of wood used to iron bolts of fabric) were sometimes given elaborate shapes; this horse stands in front of a subtly decorated wall on a Folldal farm (preceding pages).

abruptly from sunshine to freezing cold. Despite its fickleness, April remains a momentous month, a time of rebirth which has, not surprisingly, inspired Norwegian poets. Nobel Prize winner Bjørnstjerne Bjørnson—a contemporary of Ibsen and as exuberant an extrovert as Ibsen was an introvert—wrote a particularly famous poem about this month.

Because Norway extends over such a vast latitude, spring arrives at very different times across the 1,750 kilometres of mountains, fields and forests separating the sunny southern coast of the Sørlandet from the sparse highland forest on the northern border, between the county of Finmark and the ex-Soviet Union. While Laplanders celebrate their Easter wedding festivities in the snow up north, southerners are already well into their spring rites. Poet Nils Collett Vogt wrote of 'winter's loss' and 'spring's victory' in his 1917 poem *Homecoming*, and we understand exactly what he means.

For Mr Arne Steckmest of the renowned Bergen shipping family, spring at the aristocratic 1732 Erviken villa (top) means opening terrace doors that lead towards the extensive gardens and moorings where the family motorboat is ready to start the season. In western Norway, the Gulf Stream brings an early spring to the gardens; on the Hardanger fjord (above), on the Sognefjord (right) and on the Oslo fjord (left) whose light dazzled Monet.

EDVARD GRIEG'S HOUSE. If you want an early spring, the place to find it is on the stretch of ragged coastline of the prosperous old commercial town of Bergen. Here, the Caribbean-tempered waters of the Gulf Stream sweep in from across the Atlantic Ocean. Nestling among hills, Bergen has been a major trade centre since the Hanseatic League, the mid-14th century organization of towns formed to protect and control trade. Bergen was home to composer Edvard Grieg and enjoys a thriving cultural life. Every year in May, Grieg's native city welcomes the Festspillerre, which has become most important music in Norway since it was found in 1953. During the festival, the country's cultural elite and big names from the international music circuit come together in the concert hall, the Grieghallen, and the bars and restaurants of the Norge Hotel.

Outside Bergen, by the forest-lined coast, lies Troldhaugen, or hill of the trolls, the rambling, wooden, two-storey cream-coloured villa built in 1885, where Edvard and Nina Grieg spent their springs and summers. Today, music lovers make their pilgrimage to the villa to attend concerts during the festival. Grieg married his cousin, Nina Hagerup, in 1867, and their marriage proved to be exceptionally close and loving. Not only did Nina inspire many of Grieg's songs, but she was also a fine interpreter of them. "She sang like a bird—her voice was like an inexhaustible spring," wrote a family friend. Grieg was forty-two when he and Nina took possession of Troldhaugen after years of travelling and periods of separtion. It was their first permanant home, and from 1885 onwards they came to Troldhaugen every April after spending the winter months further south.

Troldhaugen has not changed much since the Griegs lived here. Surrounded by trees, the spacious house with its large, glazed veranda and tall square flagpole-topped tower remains much as it was in the Griegs' days. Raw, unpainted wooden walls create an intimate atmosphere in the large drawing room where informal concerts were organised for friends. The furniture is designed in a simple Dragon style and the chairs are upholstered in velvet. The Steinway grand piano in the timber-walled salon was Bergen's appreciative gift for the couple's silver anniversary in 1892. Nowhere else can we feel the composer's presence so strongly as during a spring morning visit to his peaceful villa.

At the bottom of the steep path leading to the fjord lies a small wooden hut where Grieg found the tranquility necessary to compose his sensual, disturbing music. When he died in 1907, Grieg was buried close to this study, at the foot of the cliffs. Nina joined him there twenty-eight years later.

"Great composers like Bach and Beethoven have built churches and temples on the heights. I myself, just like Ibsen has said in recent plays, wanted to build houses for people where they can feel at home and live happily," said Norway's great national composer, Edvard Grieg. Not only did Grieg build "musical homes" where all Norwegians feel very much at home, but in 1884, seventeen years after their marriage, Mr Grieg and his wife, Nina, had Troldhaugen villa built, their first permanent home between travels. With its wide views (above) over the hills and the fjord, its rustic wooden walls and late 19th-century bourgeois furniture in its salon (right), Troldhaugen villa is an enchanting stopping-place in the pilgrimage across Europe's musical history.

Edvard Grieg once said about his music that he had remained a German Romantic of the Schumann school. "But at the same time, I incorporated my country's rich folk heritage, and from this as-yet unexplored realm of the Norwegian soul, I have tried to create a national art," he added. Troldhaugen's Steinway grand piano, at which he spent so many intense moments, was a gift from the town of Bergen for the Griegs' silver wedding anniversary in 1892, fifteen years before Grieg's death. The casually comfortable salon (right) is scattered with many photos, as well as memorabilia from an eventful life. Behind the piano (above) we can see a photo of Grieg. The Griegs gave delightful house concerts in the salon; the composer played, and Nina Grieg interpreted her husband's songs, all of which were written for her.

"All around, the market bustles like an allegory of Scandinavia," writes Jan Morris about Bergen's *Fiskebryggen* market. "There are stalls of prawns, pickled herring and smoked trout, trestle tables piled high with potted plants and cut flowers, lobsters scuttling about in tanks and men gutting huge salmons in the sunshine. There are women selling reindeer pelts and cucumbers and boxes of mountain berries...." *Fiskebryggen*, the very symbol of old Bergen, is surpassed only by *Bryggen*. These old Hanseatic piers are bordered by elegantly aligned wooden warehouses, the centre of much of Bergen's activity, including visits of the fine old sailboat school (left) *Statsraad Lehmkuhl*. The old warehouses can be charming, as the intimate, colourful restaurant *To Kokker* (right) shows. Next door to it you find a maritime bar (below).

THE WESTERN PORTS. During the three centuries of Danish rule, Bergen was Norway's unofficial capital. During the 15th and 16th centuries, the fishermen and the powerful 'lords' of the fishing towns further north brought their trade to Bergen where the enterprising merchant aristocracy took advantage of the powerful Hansa network spanning most of northern Europe. The centre of all commercial activity was the Bryggen, or quay, the central harbour bordered by three- and four-storey wooden warehouses. Now beautifully restored, these warehouses have been converted into shops, offices and restaurants.

Many of the local traditions rooted in Bergen's medieval trading past survive today. The tough-talking street boys and the neighbourhood street bands have been part of local life for generations and enhance the lively atmosphere around the port and in the town's steep, narrow streets. Local pride for Bergen's important past still runs deep.

"I am not from Norway, I'm from Bergen," people used to say—and still do—with the characteristic burred 'r's of the Bergen dialect. The people of Bergen feel special and there is still a keen sense of rivalry with the official capital, Oslo. The town's population undeniably includes some of today's most sophisticated Norwegians, people with taste, *savoir-vivre* and a keen sense of tradition.

Bergen remains an important fishing port and you are reminded of this wherever you go. You can buy fish fresh from the fishmongers in the market square by the harbour and prepare it at home, or enjoy it in one of the intimate restaurants, such as To Kokker (the two cooks) or Enhjørningen (the Unicorn), which have been set up in the old quay-side warehouses. Inside, their rooms are small and cosy with old timber walls painted deep, vibrant colours. The wolffish *flambé* with pepper sauce or cod, boiled *au naturel*, so fresh that it curls on your plate, are particularly popular dishes.

LIVING IN OLD BERGEN. Businesswoman and interior decorater Sissel Bistrup and her husband have chosen to live in the heart of old Bergen in an elegant, little house built in 1754 on the buried ruins of the medieval Munkeliv Kloster, or monk's life monastery. The couple, who divide their time betwen their homes in Oslo and Bergen, bought the house in 1979, and it provides a peaceful, relaxing environment for a busy family. For the exterior, Mrs Bistrup chose a grey-violet colour which she had seen on a house in Holland. The interior contains bright textiles and pieces of art and furniture enthusiastically quarried from antique dealers here and there. The words 'salle à manger intime' are inscribed on the door frame of a small sitting room where the family now has its meals.

"It's an easy and practical house that sort of wraps itself around you. It is surprisingly spacious once you get inside and it provides a wonderful haven right in the middle of old Bergen's urban culture," says Mrs Bistrup. The enormous, unsigned painting in the sitting room was snapped up from a Bergen antique dealer after the original buyer could not get it through his front door. Experts say that it may be from the Tintoretto school and was probably part of a larger painting.

Prosperity from fishing and trade spread along Norway's western coasts, reaching as far as Ålesund, a small port 150 miles to the north, in the Sunnmøre area. In the past, Ålesund, like Bergen, was extensively damaged by fire; in 1904, the whole of the town centre burnt down. But the fire was a blessing in disguise because it paved the way for fine Art Nouveau buildings which have been beautifully preserved.

Hardangersøm, the traditional openwork embroideries (above) of the Hardanger fjord area, that you also find in the region's rich folk costumes, is a specialty at the antique shop Blonder og Stas in one of the old warehouses at Bryggen. Mrs Sissel Bistrup, a decorator, has combed antique shops to furnish her 1754 Bergen home, a timber house with a masonry exterior (right). It has a beautiful collection of furniture, pots, and brass pans.

Ålesund is a vibrant, prosperous old town where people enjoy the good life. In spring, everyone is drawn to the water. One of the best places from which to enjoy it is the Bryggen Hotel, a small, picturesque, informal hotel in a converted warehouse by the Hellesundet canal. On a bright spring day, the row of pastel-coloured warehouses is reflected in the harbour waters. In the next-door warehouse, the exclusive Sjø-bua Restaurant offers delicious fish or lobster dinners. These converted warehouses are attractive for many purposes, and some of them have been turned into cosy feet-in-the-water flats.

RITES OF SPRING AT AN OLD VILLA. Spring arrives earlier in Bergen than it does in the east of the country, and in the Bergen area it first appears on a narrow strip of land to the north of the town between the sea and the foot of the steep Sandviksfjellet mountain, which shields it

In Ålesund, a town built on three islands, the sea is the center of activity. The Hellesundet sound cuts through the city which is bathed in the morning sun (right). Here, the Bryggen Hotel (top) and Sjøbua Restaurant (above) have maintained their waterfront atmosphere in their restored warehouses, and on the pier (left), Tore Bjørn Skjøldsvik's 1991 sculpture *Sildekona* (The woman selling herring) reminds you that much of this prosperous town's wealth came from the fisheries.

from cold northern winds. The area contains a particularly fine example of the type of luxurious villa that the prosperous Bergen merchants had built during the 18th and 19th centuries. The white Louis XVI-style villa—Brødretomten, or brother's site, was built in 1797 as a relatively proximate summer retreat for the merchant brothers Fredrik and Henrik Meyer. It was purchased in 1959 by the parents of Anders Haaland, an historian specialising in the urban history of Bergen and Stavangar.

Bergen's merchant class became quite affluent during the French revolution and the early Napoleonic years, until Denmark was forced into the war in 1807 on Napoleon's side and pulled Norway along with it. At the time, fifty or so summer pleasure villas were set in what was then isolated countryside.

Spring at Brødretomten is a time of abundant growth and rich colour; fruit tree blossoms are followed by long rows of huge white and pink rhododendrons. The house was built for pleasure and for exclusively male parties. The spacious dining room, dominated by an impressive mural in blues and greens depicting the battle between the British and the Danes in Copenhagen harbour in 1801, can seat forty people and is the villa's most important room. Although they do not have quite the same resources as the original owners, Mr Haaland has maintained Brødretomten's traditions.

The house was modernized by the previous owner but it remains a cold place in winter. Mr Haaland grew up here and has childhood memories of water taps freezing in the 1920s bathrooms and tiles falling off the steep mansard roof. Because of the high cost of hiring professional builders and plumbers, Mr Haaland and his son have used

In spacious pleasure villas like the 1797 Brødretomten (left), a convenient boat or carriage ride from town, gentlemen from Bergen's leisure merchant classes, and important officials came together for festive dinners lasting until early morning, followed by "Bergen breakfasts" of madeira and cognac. The dining room furniture, painted in white, enhances the elegance of the room (right).

their muscle power to the full. Every three or four years he spends three hard weeks scraping and repainting the whole house. But Mr Haaland, like his parents, loves this exceptional property on the lush coastal landscape and he accepts all the work that it demands.

A VIRTUOSO'S HOUSE. The west coast of Norway exerts a powerful attraction and many people who have travelled widely return to make their permanent homes here. In 1865, after half a lifetime of triumph on both sides of the Atlantic, Ole Bull, a virtuoso violinist and popular composer of nationalistic music, hailed as Paganini's equal, built Bull-ahuset, or Bull's house, in the lush green hills north east of Bergen.

The son of a prosperous pharmacist, Bull had grown up in Bergen, but his childhood summers were spent in his grandfather's old house in the forest on the other side of the fjord. The outbreak of the American

Internationally acclaimed master violinist Ole Bull built his dream house in 1863 on the old family property in the Valestrand area just outside Bergen. Bullahuset (Bull House) was the first house designed in the highly nationalistic Viking style to be built in Scandinavia, and had a dragon riding high on the roof ridge (above). The upstairs *Høvdingesalen* or main hall (left), whose atmosphere recalls the ancient halls of local Viking chiefs, has an elaborate wooden lace decor. Bull gave house concerts here for visiting Norwegian and foreign friends. The black wicker chairs were Mr Bull's dining room chairs, and in the house's smaller hall (right), he had Italian-style twisted pillars constructed.

civil war caused Mr Bull's concert engagements on the other side of the Atlantic to dwindle, giving him more time to devote to building a new summer house on the old family property. Bull had met and married his French wife, Félicité Villeminot-Bull, in Paris during his triumphant youth. She had not at all appreciated his long absences or the irregularity of his pay-cheques and was less than enthusiastic about old Valestrand, preferring to live in Oslo. Ironically, she did not survive to see her husband's new home: she died three years before the completion of Bullahuset, the first romantic Dragon Viking building to be built in Scandinavia. After her death, Ole Bull took a second foreign wife—an American—built another house, which he called Lysøen, and was saved from bankruptcy by his rich American father-in-law. Lysøen, on the southern outskirts of Bergen, was designed along the same lines as Bullahuset and is now the Bull Museum.

Today, Bullahuset, with its clean-lined white exterior, Viking dragons and Swiss-style eaves' carvings and strikingly ornate wooden interior, belongs to Bull's great-great-grandson, Knut Hendriksen, a director at the Stockholm Opera. Mr Hendriksen spent his childhood summers at Valestrand and spends as much time at Bullahuset as his busy opera schedule permits. He is conscious of the place which the house occupies in Norway's cultural history and the obligations it brings. The rest of the year, helping hands keep up Bullahuset's agricultural activities, chiefly cow and sheep farming.

THE ROCOCO SPLENDOURS OF DAMSGÅRD. Many of Bergen's most remarkable houses are private residences, but fortunately some of the town's most beautiful wooden mansions have been turned into public foundations administered by the Vestlandske Kunstindustrimuseum, so that everyone can admire them. Overlooking the bay leading in to Bergen's inner harbour lies the finest of them all, Norway's most elegant and best preserved Rococo building, Damsgård manor. Built in 1700, on a smaller scale but in a similar style to palaces around Europe, Damsgård used to be a grand summer house, a stage for lavish parties thrown for Bergen's elite. From 1870 on, successive owners lived in the house year round until the state, in conjunction with the Bergen City Council, acquired the property in 1983. Since then, the conservation of Damsgård has been a major priority for the authorities responsible for historic buildings and the house is open to the public during the spring and summer.

The building is U-shaped, with two wings forming a courtyard to the rear, and has an exquisite rococo facade. There are two storeys

Damsgård manor's superb *Blåstuen* (Blue salon) has strikingly elegant blue and white wallpaper imported from England around 1770, and fine 18th-century chairs in Bergen rococo (above) in front of the towering secretary. Damsgård was built largely between 1770 and 1780, and is Norway's finest rococo building. The house was designed to host large, luxurious parties for the Bergen aristocracy and prosperous commercial classes, and has four elegant salons. Such a house required a considerable cooking capacity, so Damsgård has two kitchens which have now been restored to their original colours (right).

and the upper floor is reached by a porticoed staircase with marbled red and grey balusters. The central section of Damsgård dates back to the early 18th century, but the building took on its present form towards the end of the century on the initiative of its owner, War Commissioner J. C. Geelmuyden Gyldenkrantz. Subsequent owners extended the buildings around the paved courtyard and added touches of their own, but Damsgård remains an exquisite example of rococo architecture. Indeed, Damsgård exemplifies Bergen's rococo style, which tends to be richer and 'fatter' than the inland versions.

In the past, collecting porcelain was a sign of wealth and Damsgård's guests—who often came by boat from their Bergen townhouses—would usually be led through the room where the porcelain collection was displayed, so that they would have a chance to admire it before moving on to the four drawing rooms where social events took place. Arranged symmetrically on either side of the central tower, each of these drawing rooms preserves its original wallpaper and each has its own particular atmosphere although all have walls and ceilings of superb rococo design. The most opulent room is the upstairs hall, decorated with rich green wallpapers and black drapes. The furnishings are correspondingly lavish: 18th-century sideboards and chandeliers, and early 18th-century chairs covered in gilt leather or late 18th-century Hepplewhite. On the walls hang portraits of past owners of the house, while between the windows, two large Empire mirrors enhance the sumptuous decor. As in many 18th-century residences, the lady and the master had their chambers at opposite ends of the main building, each opening on to a private garden—the lady's to the west, with duck and carp ponds and the master's to the east, laid out in a more formal design.

Damsgård's gardens have been restored to their original state, while inside, the lady's bedroom has regained its delightful, feminine atmosphere. Its walls are covered in iridescent, silky, early 19th-century red, pink, yellow and orange wallpapers, and there is a canopy bed with red printed cotton curtains from the end of the 18th century. The master's bedroom has been restored to its 1900 decor and is altogether simpler, with walls covered in light green painted canvas. Now that the years of meticulous conservation work are over, Damsgård's splendours can be admired by us all.

A FAMOUS PAPER MILL. Not far from Damsgård stands Alvøen, once the idyllic home of the 'paper baron' Fasmer. Alvøen has been turned into a museum, but it is still used by the Fasmer family on important

Damsgård (top), the exquisite rococo manor now transformed into a museum, is situated at the exit of Bergen's port.
Alvøen's neighbouring villa, ancient property of the Fasmer family, is open to the public. In this peaceful, sheltered Renaissance garden, seated on one of these small benches (above), or in the summer pavillion (right), you really feel spring coming in this serene landscape on Bergen's outskirts.

Aristocrats and artists came together at Kvikne's hotel when it opened in 1887 (top). Renowned landscape painters like Hans Dahl and Adelsten Normann met foreign colleagues here who had also come to paint. Holland's young Queen Wilhelmina, a talented water-colourist, came to Kvikne for years. Today, a quiet breakfast is taken in a Dragon style salon (above), while from your room's lace-lined balcony, you can enjoy magnificent views over the fjord (left).

family occasions. Stylishly informal rooms in the low wooden buildings and the seaside garden laid out in a Renaissance design create a relaxed, peaceful atmosphere, which is slightly ironic when you recall that the family actually produced gunpowder until the late 19th century.

Alvøen's green drawing room is particularly delightful, with its elegant birch Empire and Biedermeier furniture, Venetian chandeliers and lush French 19th-century wallpapers featuring hunting scenes. Pantry shelves display Wedgwood china from the 1780s and fine 18th-century Norwegian glasses. An 18th-century Chinese service fills *Alvøen's* porcelain room—the only complete porcelain room remaining in Norway. The library, with its collection of 17th- and 18th- century scientific and religious books, leads out onto the front lawn separating the house from a charming six-sided pavilion. The pavilion's ceiling is painted a beautiful blue and is studded with bright golden stars.

Alvøen's famous paper mill is nearby. It is Norway's oldest mill, dating from 1797, and the only one to have produced rag-paper. Over the years it produced the paper for Norway's banknotes but was closed down in 1981 and is not open to the public. A limited amount of paper is left, among it a quantity of Alvøen's well-known, heavy, yellowish '1797' writing paper that everyone in Norway buys, making the name a household word.

HOLIDAY NOSTALGIA. Few areas in Norway are more spectacular than the Sognefjorden, Norway's longest fjord, cutting inland for 180 kilometres into the dramatic mountains and glaciers north of Bergen. During the dark part of the year, the high mountains block out the sun, but when spring and summer come to Sognefjorden it is easy to see why many regard this as Norway's most beautiful waterway. Today, tourists from around the world flock to follow in the footsteps of the European aristocracy who used to come here. Roads are few and far between in this region and ferries offer the best means of transportation.

On the Balestrand peninsula, where the ferry comes round a bend in the fjord, lies the Victorian Kvikne's Hotel. Built in 1887, this is one of the last surviving old wooden hotels in western Norway. British lords stayed here at the turn of the century and the Dragon-style lounges are redolent of the epoch's refinement and leisure. Guests can look out from their rooms' large, ornate balconies onto an impressive vista over the fjord.

Following the fjord northwards, you eventually arrive at the small village of Fjærland, where Jostedalsbreen glacier's melting freshwater colours the fjord green. It is a fitting site for Norway's new glacier museum, designed by architect professor Sverre Fehn. Here, the scale of the landscape dwarfs you, and the thought of all that frozen water just above is dizzying. At Fjærland, another evocative, nostalgic hotel from the 'English days,' the Mundal Hotel has survived. Its spacious wooden verandas and the quiet, old fashioned lounges are ideal places to recuperate from a day spent up by the glacier or walking along the fjord.

High, ragged mountains line the Sognefjorden, whose numerous narrow arms cut their way deeper and deeper into the landscape. By the side of one of these arms, a road climbs up to a spectacular hairpin bend at Stalheim—a name which comes from the old Norwegian word *stadall*, meaning resting place. Spring is the best time to visit Stalheim: life is starting up again, the roads are open to traffic and the Stalheim Hotel is open for the season. The old Stalheim hotel was destroyed by fire in 1959, and a modern hotel has been built in its place with magnificent views of the surrounding mountains and a nearby waterfall. A few yards away lies owner Mr Kaare Tønneberg's private museum , called Fuglehaugen, the bird hill, which he gladly shows to hotel guests. The museum consists of some twenty houses, the oldest and finest of which dates from the 17th century. This lovely, white-panelled, two-storey house stands at the centre of the group, and it has the same roots as Mr Tønneberg himself, since it comes from the nearby Voss area which is today an attractive ski resort. Mr Tønneberg had the house moved to a new life at Stalheim and went on to fill its rooms with precious baroque, rococo and Empire antiques. Some of the timber walls are painted in strong colours, while others are covered in fine, old wallpapers. The kitchen is a delight, with its large white fireplace, red timber walls and shining copper utensils.

A ROOM WITH A VIEW. For all their majesty, mountains and fjords can be oppressive. Ibsen explored this idea in his play *The Lady from the Sea*, in which the heroine, Ellida, finds the fjords unbearably suffocating in contrast with the vast, open expanse of the sea, with its perpetual movement and invigorating salt air. And where better to appreciate the beauty of the sea than from a lighthouse? The Høyevarde lighthouse on Karmøy Island has become an unusual holiday home for the clients and guests of Norsk Hydro, its owners.

The original lighthouse dates back to 1700 and was the third oldest in the country. Today's towering white structure was built in the 1850s, but since 1902, there has been no lighthouse keeper at Høyevarde, which functions automatically. Norsk Hydro, Norway's largest conglomerate, arranges for clients and guests to stay at Høyevarde and enjoy its simple maritime furnishings and the fresh sea air. In stormy

Out by the southwest coast, Norsk Hydro's Høyevarde lighthouse on Karmøy island (top) is idyllic on a quiet spring day. But the sea and winds can be violent in this area, and guests are relieved to find boots and oilskins in the entrance (above). Inside the Fjærland arm of Sognefjorden, Mundal Hotel (right) is another of the rambling old fjord hotels that prospered due to the patronage of British travellers. Today, glacier climbers and fishing enthusiasts relax on its peaceful veranda after a long day outdoors.

weather, Hydro's guests can put on the brightly coloured oilskins hanging in the hallway to walk from one house to the other, or they can stay indoors and watch the sea from the small window bay where the pilot used to keep a lookout for ships.

A **RENOVATED HOUSE BY THE HARDANGERFJORD.** The landscape of the Hardangerfjord south of Bergen is just as impressive as the Sognefjorden, but less threatening. This is Norway's main fruit-producing area and in the springtime the landscape explodes into a profusion of feather-light white and pink blooms. Skrivergården (the district magistrate's house) is one of the finest houses in the area. It was restored by Arild Haaland, who renovated Brødretomten in Bergen which is now in the hands of his son Anders. Arild Haaland, a philosopher at Bergen University and one of Norway's more colourful public figures,

Stalheim's dramatically beautiful mountainside hides an architectural treasure: Mr Kaare Tønneberg's large, panelled 1726 house. Close to his Stalheim hotel, this house has strong 18th-century interior colours which contrast sharply with its gleaming white exterior. The thick timber walls of the hallway (above), with its green baroque entrance door, are painted in the same strong red of the wallpapers in the adjoining large salon, furnished with urban antiques. Upstairs, the ravishing spring green salon (right) is furnished with Biedermeier, Sheraton, and Hepplewhite furniture and a late 18th-century Scottish piano.

is a tireless campaigner in controversial national heritage battles. He has renovated a number of old houses, most of them in Stavangar or on flat, barren Jæren, south of Stavangar. Skrivergården is his finest house and holds a special place in his affections.

Part baroque, part rococo, Skrivergården was built in 1723 on the Hesthamar shores of the Hardangerfjord, a boat ride away from Bergen. Johan Sechmann Fleischer, its builder, accompanied the evangelist Hans Egede on his first expedition to Greenland in 1728. Later, Mr Fleischer settled near Bergen, where he worked as a magistrate and grew steadily richer, acquiring on average two farms per year. He was the forefather of one of Norway's best known civil servant families.

After Fleischer's death, Skrivergården suffered mixed fortunes. From the 1870s until the late 1950s it was a poorhouse, and for the next fifteen years it was left empty. In 1974 the house, in a poor state,

On Hardanger fjord, Skrivergården's (magistrate's house) fifteen rooms have retained their simple and welcoming style. The blossoming flowers, signalling the arrival of spring (left), add a refreshing touch to the kitchen corner. In order to obtain a baroque style for the entrance door (right), Mr Arild Haaland and his friends hand-mixed different shades of red to create the perfect colour which matches the roof tiles. At the end of the garden, the ancient *stabbur* (stable) on the water's edge (above) sits next to Kirsten Kokkin's sculpture *Pa Flukt* (Fleeing).

was bought by the philosopher enthusiast Mr Haaland. "What saved the fine old architectural details was probably the fact that there was no money for repairs during the poorhouse years," he explains.

Since he acquired Skrivergården, restoration work has been continuous and Mr Haaland has done much of the manual work himself. The house has fifteen rooms, a portico with a fine, baroque front door, and hand-planed, wooden detailing everywhere. Everything has been meticulously restored and the traditional colours respected. His perseverance and hard work have paid off, and today Skrivergården is a delight. Every detail of the house has some kind of story attached to it and Mr Haaland enjoys sharing his intimate knowledge of the place. He has a sharp eye for form and colour and a keen appreciation of beauty in all its forms. In spring, he decorates his tables with branches from the flowering fruit trees and lilac bushes in his garden and wild flowers picked in the meadows.

In addition to flowers, of course, spring brings with it milder temperatures and a welcome respite from the cold. During the winter, confides Mr Haaland, the best place to have your breakfast is actually inside the huge, bright blue fireplace in the kitchen, with the small table pushed right under the hood to be as close as possible to the hearth and the small iron oven plates around it. Now that he intends to spend a greater part of the year here, Mr Haaland realizes he will have to do something to stop the freezing winds from rising through the kitchen floor. The hard work never ends.

THE HOUSE AT THE END OF THE FJORD. To live in the country in western Norway, you must be able to cope with two things: solitude and darkness. Imagine two small red dots that turn out to be houses at the end of a long, deep fjord, surrounded by pine-covered hills and high jagged snow-topped mountains. Those dots are Rossvoll, home of author Olav H. Hauge and his artist wife Bodil Cappelen. Rossvoll lies at the bottom of the Hardangerfjord, near the Hardangerjøkul glacier, which rises to an altitude of 1,876 metres. Their remote location provides the couple with the peace and seclusion they need for their work.

Inside the house, the small, spartan rooms are filled with books and paintings. Bodil Cappelen works on her figurative paintings while her husband writes poetry. Olav Hauge's work is published both in Norway and in English-speaking countries, and in addition to writing poetry, he also translates the work of French poets such as Rimbaud, Verlaine and René Char into Norwegian. The couple's home life is literally rooted in the soil here where they grow their own vegetables and fruit without

Mr Arild Haaland (top) has done most of the extensive restoration work on his ancient home himself, and is enthusiastically seeking out other historically interesting houses to renovate. With his keen aesthetic sense, he has designed a charming still life made of blue and white cups, an old scale, and spice pots (right) to ornate a shelf in his kitchen, where one can keep warm near the huge fireplace (above).

artificial fertilizers or insecticides —only nature's own compost is permitted, for ecology is a deep conviction at Rossvoll.

Bogstad manor. Spring may come early out on the west coast, but its arrival is met with just as much enthusiasm in the rich agricultural regions, and on the banks of the fjords further to the east. The opening to the public of the aristocratic 18th-century Bogstad manor is a sure sign of the season in Oslo. This stately home, set among the fields, forests and golf links on the western outskirts of Oslo, belonged to the Anker and Egeberg families and was inhabited up until the 1950s. The owners thought it would be best to turn the house into a publicly administered foundation in order to secure the building and its grounds for future generations.

Bogstad was built in the late 18th century. Its ground floor is relatively low-ceilinged while the upper floor is spacious and grand under the huge mansard roof. The crisp, white facade towers over the lawns leading down to Bogstad lake. Inside, the rooms are filled with silks and rococo and Empire furniture, and in the main bedroom there is a large 'king's bed' whose curtains and canopy are decorated in bright red silk brocade. There is a marvellous 'farm blue' basement kitchen, which is delightfully simple but hardly what you could describe as an efficient place to cook. In the spring, the nearby forests and meadows provide a rich and invigorating backdrop to the formal elegance of Bogstad.

When spring explodes and the fruit trees are in bloom, it is pleasant to stop and have a coffee on a slate table in the stone-walled garden (above). A feel for nature and a simple life: these are the key elements for the poet Olav H. Hauge and the painter Bodil Cappelen (left), the owners of Rossvol (right), which is located on Hardanger fjord's green riverbanks. Like them, many Norwegian artists have chosen to live in these magnificent isolated spots while still keeping in touch with the artistic community.

Upon entering the aristocratic Bogstad manor, one has the impression of walking onto a film set, and is impressed by the Louis XVI salons with their Empire and rococo styles intact. Bogstad was finished between 1760 and 1762 but its rich and powerful owner, Peder Anker, enlarged it in 1780, thereby giving the estate its current form.

On the wall of the enormous Louis XVI ballroom (left), we can see the late 18th-century paintings acquired in Peder Anker's travels. The crystal chandelier and the furniture are contemporaries of the manor. We also find four large canvases of the Guardi brothers—the only Norwegian Guardi's—depicting scenes from roman myths. Occasionally, Peder Anker ceded his 18th-century canopy bed (above) to visiting heads of state.

A PINK PALACE FOR A YOUNG FAMILY. The present Egeberg generation live at Skinnarbøl, a stamped earth mansion begun in 1809, and set in the tranquil area of forests and lakes outside the town of Kongsvinger in southeast Norway. During a fifteen-year period towards the end of the 1814-1905 Swedish-Norwegian union, Queen Sophie, wife of King Oscar II, spent her holidays at Skinnarbøl.

Because of the queen's regular visits until the union ended, Skinnarbøl was often called 'the frontier palace', and its strict pink Empire facade and distinctive portico does indeed resemble that of the larger Royal Palace at Oslo. The locations of the two palaces, however, could not be more different. While Oslo's Royal Palace overlooks the busy, sloping Karl Johan Street, (named for Sweden/Norway's early 19th-century monarch), Skinnarbøl has wide views over a lake and gentle, forest-covered hills.

In 1983, the younger generation of the Egeberg family, Pernille and Westye Egeberg and their three sons, took over Skinnarbøl from Westye's parents. The energetic Egebergs use the entire property and manage the place without any extra help. More than thirty rooms cover one thousand square metres. There are over 175 acres of cereal growing in the fields and 6000 acres of forest nearby. Pernille Egeberg finds her background as a librarian invaluable for managing a house like this, where you must be well organised. At the entrance to the house, the visitor is greeted by a huge antique sleigh filled with logs. Further on are a number of salons, some of which have whitewashed floors, and some gilded continental antiques and family portraits. The smoking room has deep, comfortable rattan armchairs, elk trophies on the walls and a large chandelier made from an antler.

"Spring is a busy time at Skinnarbøl," admits Mrs Egeberg, "there are endless tasks to attend to, such as removing innumerable wooden plugs from the foundation walls and ventilating the arcaded cellar, planting hundreds of flowering plants throughout the grounds, and preparing the vegetable garden, not to mention all the spring work in the fields."

A SENSE OF TRADITION. The idyllically located villa belonging to Tone Vigeland, Norway's most famous contemporary jewelry designer, amply demonstrates how the sea adds an extra dimension to spring. The villa is surrounded by a large, sloping garden with flowering fruit trees and has an intriguing stolen view over the Oslofjorden. A traditional, tarred building built in 1908, the house has large rooms which exude quality and tradition. The house has been owned by the Vige-

The exceptional pink facade of Skinnarbål manor (below), also called "Little Bogstad" or "the frontier palace," is a striking feature in the southwest of the country on the outskirts of Kongsvinger. When spring comes, light Grieg harmonies can be heard through open windows played on the Bechstein grand piano (left) in the music room. Firewood is at hand on the antique sleigh which was brought from the barn to the hall (right), which is beautifully crafted with a mosaic tile floor.

land family since it was built and the interior reflects the artistic sensibilities of the different generations who have lived here. The light, painted walls of the downstairs rooms are filled with contemporary etchings and urban antiques while the upstairs rooms have a more rustic feel, with old farm furniture and wide views over the garden and the fjord beyond.

Pieces of Mrs Vigeland's unsentimental, sculptural metal jewelry have been acquired by the Museum of Modern Art and the Cooper-Hewitt Museum in New York, London's Victoria and Albert Museum, Tokyo's Museum of Modern Art, and various museums and private collections throughout Scandinavia and Germany. Her work contrasts sharply with the quiet, traditional house she and her family live in. Her upstairs studio is filled with tools and an intriguing array of raw materials disposed along the white walls. These small pieces of metal

eventually turn up at jewelry exhibitions and museums as components of large, intricate, bristling cascades that seem to cling to your body and move with you.

Small, restless and slender, Mrs Vigeland stands firmly on her own two feet, depite her significant artist family. Her grandfather was the nationally-known sculptor Emmanuel Vigeland, and his brother, Gustav Vigeland, was an internationally known sculptor whose massive granite and bronze figures stand in Oslo's Vigeland sculpture park, created for his work. Tone Vigeland's father, Per Vigeland, was a painter. The house remains much as grandfather Vigeland left it, except for some modern, feminine touches and the numerous etchings and paintings given to Mrs Vigeland by her friends and colleagues in Norway's contemporary art community. Here and there you come across one of her sensuous little sculptures casually hung on a wall or banister.

"Living here I feel the peace, the quality of life, and the sense of tradition very deeply. It is so different from what is usually built today," she says, nestling into one of the armchairs beside the stocks of firewood on the upstairs balcony under the eaves. "In spring, when this beautiful old garden comes alive again, you can lie in a hammock stretched between the fruit trees and while away the days like a lizard." The garden has long, sloping lawns and beside the house are the sizzling waters of her grandfather's sculpture fountain *The Virgin and the Unicorn*, similar to the one in Nygård Park in Bergen. Grandfather Vigeland's large studio, which has been turned into a museum lies behind the trees. On this side of the trees, however, the Vigeland's way of life is definitely a contemporary one.

Edvard munch's fisherman's cabin. When May slides into June, outdoor life heats up, particularly on the edge of the Oslofjorden, in little towns like Asgårdstrand. It was in this popular place for artists that Edvard Munch painted most of his best known paintings, turning the landscape of rock, water, beach and trees into emblems of his alienation and yearning. 'Wandering here is like walking around among my paintings. I get such an urge to paint here in Asgårdstrand," wrote Munch to the art collector Rolf Stenersen, who described his friendship with Munch in his 1946 book *Close up of a Genius*.

Oslo may be the place to go if you want to plunge into the immense, painful drama of Munch's work—in the Munch Museum and the National Gallery—but the real and imaginary dramas unfolded in Asgårdstrand. It was here that he painted such famous canvases as *Melancholy* and *Inger on the Beach*. The motifs he returned to again

Skinnarbøl's wide sloping lawns (above), leading down to the Vingersjoen lake, provide a view treasured by Swedish-Norwegian Queen Sophie during her summers spent here until Norway's independence from Sweden in 1905. The elk-head trophies and the antique guns in the casually comfortable Smoking Room (right) remind you that Skinnarbøl is located in the middle of huge hunting areas that are filled with elk, deer, hare, beaver and forest birds.

and again—of women standing on the pier or among the beachside trees, and of men and women dancing by the shore—were inspired by the landscape at Asgårdstrand.

Munch first came here in the summer of 1889, and stayed in a rented house. Eventually, in 1897, he bought his own house, which was no more than a modest, sparsely furnished fisherman's cabin dating from the late 18th century. He installed his studio in a small barn set among the trees. Although Munch later bought two large properties elsewhere, and also at a certain point rented a manor on the opposite side of the fjord, the Asgårdstrand cottage seems to have been especially close to his heart. He called it Lykkehuset (happiness house), and later, during the 1930s, wrote to a friend "I sit in the only cosy house that I have ever lived in—the Asgårdstrand house." In his 1889 painting, *Spring*, which he painted during his first stay at Asgårdstrand, Munch depicted spring sunshine shining through freshly ironed white curtains. His image beckons us to throw ourselves into the brief, heady, bright spring at Asgårdstrand.

When spring's blossoms arrive, silversmith Tone Vigeland lazes in her hammock (left) near her grandfather Emanuel Vigeland's fountain sculpture *Jomfruen og Enhjörningen* (The Virgin and the Unicorn) in the garden of the old family villa on Oslo's residential hill (top).

"He always preferred to stay in the garden, where he could be alone and undisturbed with his own thoughts," wrote Edvard Munch around 1906, when he occupied a modest yellow fisherman's cabin in Åsgårdstrand (above). Munch refers to himself in the third person in his journals, secretly dreaming of a writing career following the example of his friend August Strindberg.

SUMMER

Midsummer's day brings in the summer season.
Endless days and white nights provide
the rhythm for seaside holidays in southern coastal
residences, log cabin mountain farms,
and in fisherman's cabins north of the Arctic Circle
in the dazzling Midnight Sun.

After months of cocooning behind closed doors, or bundled up in layers of luxurious wools when venturing outside, Norwegians throw themselves into the sun, warmth and bright nights of summer with unlimited energy. The most popular summer region is the Sørlandet, or southern country, which is the coastal belt running south from the old maritime town of Kragerø. With the coming of summer, the Sørlandet suddenly becomes the centre of the universe. The cliffs and seaside pastures are dotted with enchanting wooden houses—some old, some new—whose wood-panelled walls are painted inside and out gleaming white, bright red or yellow, and people all up and down the coast, in the idyllic bays and on the islands, open these *hytter*, or summer chalets, and set out their deck chairs by the clear, glittering sea in preparation for the lazy days to come.

Compared with the overcrowded beaches of the Mediterranean, the Sørlandet might appear relatively quiet and wonderfully secluded. But as summer gets under way, the coastline starts to buzz with activity. Life heats up in the little towns with their busy harbours and old sea captains' houses; the sea fills with bathers and boats. On 23rd June, midsummer's eve, schools close for two months and the summer bells ring. The whole coast lights up with blazing bonfires made patiently, stored up for the occasion over long months.

As idyllic and relaxing as the Sørlandet is in summer, many Norwegians still prefer the mountains, and they head off for two- or three-day hikes taking them from chalet to chalet, especially at the end of July and the beginning of August when lazing by the sea is beginning to lose its appeal. In July, the country virtually closes down and it becomes impossible to get hold of Norwegians. Even Oslo is transformed into 'holiday land' as life explodes onto café terraces, awash with the *joie de vivre* that summer's arrival brings. The days seem to be endless, doors and windows remain open and people serve their friends delicious dinners of fresh boiled salmon, cucumber salads and huge bowls of strawberries (which taste sweeter in Norway than anywhere else). Evenings are spent outdoors around huge plates laden with seafoods including succulent fresh shrimps and mussels, which people buy in the harbours or collect themselves at the foot of the white cliffs.

As the days get longer, nobody wants to go to bed. In the south, it is possible to read outside in the garden until eleven o'clock at night and the sun is already up again by four in the morning. North of the Arctic Circle, the sun doesn't set at all, creating an almost unreal atmosphere. During these 'white' nights of the midnight sun, time seems to stand still. To enjoy the beauty of the midnight sun at its most breathtaking,

Sunset in a fiery summer sky on the Sørlandet coast (preceding pages) above the 1750 former tap-room house, now the luxurious summer home of an Oslo shipping family. Further up Norway's most sought after summer coastal area, where midsummer's night is celebrated on June 23rd by bonfires and cliffside dances, holiday-makers bask in the sun (left). Rekefabrikken (The Shrimp factory), an art gallery in the old fishing-village of Nevlunghavn. In Oslo's inner harbour, people buy fresh fish and shrimp directly from the fisherman's boat (below).

the place to be is a spartan, weatherbeaten, red fisherman's cabin up in the Lofoten archipelago or in the dramatic scenery of the North Cape.

In Norway, our summer dreams have all the space they need. Holiday homes are often hundreds of metres apart and there is an intense feeling of freedom, of being part of a pure and comforting landscape where gentle cliffs are continuously washed by the waves. The water is so clear that you can see crabs and starfish on the sea bed. You can take your boat out to one of the small, bare islands or reefs that are scattered on the sea and sunbathe from morning till evening with only the seabirds looking on as you break for an occasional cooling dip.

Numerous summer events lure people away from their beaches and islands. One of the biggest of these is the wooden boat festival which takes place in August in the little port of Risør. Here, enthusiasts from far and near, people who love the sight and sound of finely honed, varnished wood on water, gather in their sailboats and motorboats. The little harbour teems with boats and aficionados move from deck to deck, turning the festival into one enormous party, an exuberant celebration of saltwater camaraderie.

Many artists and craftspeople have settled on the Sørlandet coast and in summer the small, informal arts and crafts galleries are full of holidaymakers. The Rekefabrikken (the shrimp factory) occupies a tiny yellow building on a rock inside Nevlunghavn harbour. As the name suggests, the building used to be a shrimp processing factory, but now it is a summer gallery selling watercolours and craft products as well as creamy waffles, to holidaymakers coming ashore.

The Sørlandet is rich in fine, 18th- and 19th-century fishermen's and captains' houses, but Lyngør, an immaculately preserved old sea pilot and customs station south of Risør, is an exceptionally pretty fishing village. With its small, white, wooden houses built on the rocks around three inlets, Lyngør is so striking that it was named 'best preserved place in Europe 1991' by an international tourism jury.

For most of the year, Lyngør, which actually consists of three separate islands, claims no more than around one hundred inhabitants, but in summer it is one of the Sørlandet's most sought-after locations. It is idyllic and romantic, and hardly changed since the days of sailing ships. The port, lined with one-or two-storey houses, swarms with boats, as adults and children make the most of their precious sunny seaside days. Here, boats are far more than just leisure toys, on the contrary they provide the only means of transport between Lyngør's islands. From a very early age, children get used to handling seacraft and their bodies quickly become atuned to the sensuous rhythm of the waves.

Along Norway's southeastern coast the climate is sometimes so mild that even herbs like thyme, cultivated on the terrace to flavour summer meals, survive the winter (above). One of summer's highlights on the Sørlandet is the *Trebåtfestivalen* (Wooden Boat Festival) (right) which takes place in August in the fine little sailboat town of Risør, whose harbour is lined with white wooden houses. Timber trade with Holland led to the creation of Risør in the 17th century, and it grew to become an important trade and ship-building port in the 18th century without ever losing its charming small-town atmosphere.

While the cold parts of the year mean time spent indoors in warm and elaborately furnished houses, summer vacations along the Sørlandet coast mean outdoor life in the sun and water. Appropriately, indoor furnishings in old fishermen's houses or modern cabins are kept casually simple. Mrs Else Stange of Oslo has decorated the sunlit rooms of the family's sea-pilot home on a Kragerø island clifftop (right) with romantic French wallpaper and bright white furniture. Roses grow among the rocks (below) down by the children's and grandchildren's red house next to the Stanges' pier while swans swim peacefully by with their young (left). The sea is so fresh and clear in these waters that you can see the mussels and crabs on the bottom.

A SEA PILOT'S CLIFFTOP HOME. In the days of sailboats, the pilot and his family had Høyevarde (high beacon) Island to themselves. Today, Høyevarde and the neighbouring islands off Kragerø, three hours south of Oslo, form one of Norway's most sought after holiday areas. For the last twenty-eight years, the island's gently sloping cliffs and red and white houses have been a summer paradise for three generations of Oslo's Stange family.

The pilot's house stands atop the cliffs. Inside, its small but airy rooms are painted a strong blue or covered in French dog rose wallpapers in delicate shades of green and blue. The rattan and lyed-wood furniture and the dyed woven rugs help create a relaxed, informal atmosphere. Down by the wide, concrete jetties stand two little red buildings in a cosy waterfront cluster: the house, with its wide wooden sun decks and yellow roses, and the boathouse on the stone pier are now used by the children and the grandchildren.

The Stanges take full advantage of their island location, idling away the days among the rocks polished smooth by a combination of Ice Age erosion and the relentless wind and waves, or basking in the sun on wide cement decks. Sometimes they take trips around the nearby islands and reefs in their small fjord craft or their 1950s fishing boat. For the last four or five years, swans have been coming to the island to breed and there are hundreds of eider duck nests. For that reason, the Stanges never bring their dog to the island until after midsummer's

eve, by which time breeding has finished. Here, nature definitely has the last word.

When the children were small, Else Stange, a cheerful, vivacious woman with strong artistic interests, used to spend the whole summer on the island. Now it varies but the Stanges usually come for the whole of July and part of June and August. Mrs Stange and her husband, Einar, even spent the winter at Høyevarde one year, but until recently, living conditions were fairly primitive: they were without electricity and they had to draw water from a well. Now, there is a plumbing system and an electrical system. For all its charm, however, Høyevarde faces strong competition for the Stanges' affections. To say that the family is not short of holiday homes would be an understatement. Mr Stange loves buying houses and he currently owns six. His most recent acquisition is a property near Vannes in Brittany.

An old inn at water's edge. The large, white, two-storey house standing on an island off Lillesand, which is now the summer home of an Oslo shipping family, was neither a sea pilot nor a fisherman's home. It was built around 1750 as an inn and taproom. At the time, the North Sea was a thriving centre for trade and the island provided a winter haven for some forty to fifty ships before they set sail again when the ice broke open in the spring. Because the harbour was so busy and there was little space, the inn was built on the water, or, to be more precise, on a stone jetty in the bay. Inside the house a trap door reveals the unexpected sight of water and small crabs under your feet.

The island has been immortalized in the works of the early 20th-century Norwegian author Gabriel Scott. The discovery of a flint axe here suggests that it was inhabited as early as the Stone Age. From the 19th century up until it was acquired by the present owner's father, it was a home for fishermen and retired sea captains. Today the family stays there between April and late October.

The house has been furnished with what the owner smilingly describes as "simple things and pseudo-Louis XVI furniture." The interior is far from simple, however. In fact, from the moment you step into the entrance hall you realize that the house is quite remarkable, with its rough, white timber walls and its steep, wooden 'ship's stairs.' The pure, simple architectural lines of the house provide a discreet, sculptural setting for some charming maritime antiques, such as an old, green sailor's chest, a Norwegian naval split flag, and a Dutch map of the 17th century port. There was much brisk trade, both legal and clandestine, with the Dutch.

From the clifftop pavilion where the sea-pilot used to sit on the look-out for ships in distress (below), an Oslo shipping family has broad views over their archipelago. In their white, classic 1750 main house, the hall is elegantly naval (right). Sørlandet's native author, Vilhelm Krag, enjoys his idyllic waterside summer home on Ny Hellesund island, Havbukta, (bottom) a fine example of this coast's early 19th-century architectural heritage.

The light, welcoming dining room has yellow walls and a white, beamed ceiling. The furniture shows how foreign influences were introduced in these old trade ports. There is a strict, white Louis XVI style table with matching chairs and sideboard while in a corner stands an imposingly simple red Danish armoire dating from 1780. In the main sitting room, prints and models of old sailing ships are displayed on wood-panelled walls painted a delicate pink to create a warm, bright, refined atmosphere. There are old sea chests and a writing desk with drawers in blues and reds. Outside, near the cliff behind the house, a large golden lion seems to be squaring up to a modern metal sculpture by Bertoia.

High up on the cliffs stand two small, white wooden pavilions whose big windows on all sides offer an unbroken view of the sea and the neighbouring islands. The pilot used to sit in one of them, on the look-out for ships that might need guiding through the treacherous reefs. The pavilions, now furnished in white rattan, are the family's favourite place on stormy days, when the wild sea and the roaring wind create the most extraordinary spectacle.

Down below by the pier nestles a large swimming pool discreetly carved into the rock, its waters as clear and blue as the sea a stone's throw away. What makes the family decide whether to swim in the sea or in the pool? "The number of jellyfish in the sea that particular day!" laughs the owner.

THE POET'S HOUSE IN THE SØRLANDET. The ultimate dream for many Norwegians is to own a house on the Sørlandet coast, a white sea pilot or captain's house, with its neat, four-pane windows filled by light curtains and huge pots of red geraniums. These small but discreetly comfortable houses tend to have a standard layout. A low front doorway leads into a panelled entrance hall. Off one side of the hall is a wall-papered dining room and off the other a sitting room. At the end is the kitchen, a clean, simple room whose walls are decorated with the family's copper utensils and the pottery the captain brought back from his travels. Steep, ship-like stairs lead up to the bedrooms which are tucked under the eaves. Because the bedrooms had no running water, these houses are a veritable gold mine for collectors of faïence and stoneware mugs and wash bowls.

Over the years, the captains, pilots and fishermen vacated these houses, more or less voluntarily, moving to more practical and more centrally located homes. As they became available, the old houses were snapped up by city dwellers and until a few years ago they could still

One piece of splendid furniture can make even the simplest room striking. Such is the case with this bedroom in Havbukta's little waterside annex (right), where this antique box bed embellishes the space. This piece, with its blue, golden-starred "sky", probably comes from the Setesdal valley. Life and literature at Havbukta were mixed to such a degree that Mr Krag let Major von Knarren, one of his excentric characters, sleep here. Havbukta is strongly linked to the North Sea shipping culture, which is represented by its colour scheme of whites, blues and greens (above).

be bought at moderate prices. But now, a house with its own beach and pier costs millions of kroner—that is if you can find one to buy, for these charming houses tend to be kept in the family and passed on from generation to generation.

Those who were not able to buy a house on the Sørlandet coast built one, and the bays and islands are dotted with modern, one-storey holiday chalets. These are generally simple little wooden buildings, painted inside and out in bright colours, whose main function is to provide accommodation as close to the sea as possible. Before the late 1960s, it was still possible to build at the water's edge, but since then, the law has since become more democratic and it is forbidden to build less than one hundred metres from the water. Beaches remain accessible to everyone this way, even to those who cannot afford to own a house in the Sørlandet.

If you had to choose one house to symbolize the sensuous life in the Sørlandet it would probably be Havbukta (ocean bay) on an island in the Ny Hellesund sound between Mandal and Kristiansand. It is hardly surprising that Havbukta incarnates all that is best about life in the Sørlandet, because it was Vilhelm Krag's home, the writer whose name will always be inseparably linked to the region. It was Krag who actually coined the name Sørlandet, and to Norwegians, the mere mention of the author immediately conjures up images of a brilliant sun hanging over small, white, clifftop houses with wild, colourful, flower-filled gardens bounded by white wooden fences, philosophical old fishermen, small town eccentrics, and the little ladies of the local bourgeoisie

When Vilhelm Krag died in 1933, the house was inherited by his youngest son, Preben Kielland Krag, who spent summers there with his wife, Gynt, an Oslo architect, and their chidren. The family has kept the house much as it was, preserving the colour scheme of strong sea greens and blues, the antique, English floral wallpaper, the Hogarth prints and old birchwood and mahogany furniture. Although they take good care of the house, the family does not want it to become a cult place. For them, it is first and foremost a summer home, a place for wonderful family holidays.

Havbukta, with its sixty acres of cliffs and greenery, was built in 1864 and donated to Vilhelm Krag by the prosperous citizens of the area. Krag, who lived there for half of the year, cherished the house and continually made improvements to it driven by his good taste and aesthetic sense. Havbukta came to life in Krag's poetry, notably in *Songs from my Island*, written in 1918. The house actually consists of three little houses together with a poet's hut hidden among the trees, away

During Norway's long summer vacations, from Midsummer until well into August, people spend their time out on the sea or happily entrenched on their little island, which has become the centre of the universe. People travel by boat to visit each other during long outdoor evenings, and the sunset and tomorrow's weather is all that matters. Outside Kragerø, three generations of an industrialist's family spend summers on their large, private island in their grand 1720 white main house with its clean lines (above) and red mid-19th century barn. One generation has made its summer headquarters in the barn, with its colourful 1920's ceiling decorations (right). Sørlandet summers can bring rain, so the dining-table is long enough to receive both family and friends under the iron lamp, that was specially made based on old drawings. Properties like this very rarely come on the market since they are passed on from generation to generation. Those who have always spent their childhood summer vacations here cannot imagine summer anywhere else.

from the hubbub of family life. Today, boats pass in front of Havbukta's wooden gate with its sun-inspired design, just as they did in Krag's time.

Inland, the houses tend to be decorated in more earthy colours, but here on the coast, people are inspired by the sky and the sea and prefer strong, unexpected greens and blues. In this respect, Havbukta, as Mrs Krag points out, is basically no different from the other seamen's houses on the Sørlandet coast. Like them, Havbukta has large grounds which in those days was not a sign of wealth but merely reflected the fact that the coast was not sought after. Over the years, the Krags have donated some twenty-five acres of their land to the public so that, true to the spirit of Vilhelm Krag, other people can enjoy the charms of the Ny Hellesund area.

SUMMER QUARTERS IN A RED BARN. Perhaps the most desirable properties on the Sørlandet coast are the big, old, Empire houses. Some stand on extensive clifftop grounds, others are surrounded by forest. Some occupy whole islands to themselves. Not surprisingly, these magnificent properties rarely come on the market—when you've got the best, you do not willingly let go of it.

One of these large, luxurious houses stands discreetly among the trees on a lush, green island off Kragerø. Here, three generations of a family come together for holidays. The younger generation have taken over the large, white 1720 main house with its yellow windows and deep green double doors at the top of the stone stairs leading down to the lawns. The red barn dates from the 1850s and has richly decorated, steeply sloping ceilings. It was transformed into an informal but elegant summer home by the grandmother.

On the day school closes, a streamer is hoisted to the top of the flagpost where it stays until school starts again, on 20th August. Reunited, the family enjoys all the pleasures of life by the sea. They can play golf on their own nine-hole course and there is a red clay tennis court where the traditional family tournament is held. Much time and effort has been devoted to restoring the main house, with its light wooden summer furniture and fine old iron stoves that are used on cooler days. The most intriguing part of the property, however, is the barn. Its large, sloping ceiling is painted with acanthus motifs and figures ranging from Norwegian fishermen to scantily clad Pacific island beauties. This decoration dates back to 1925, when a member of the family bought the island and had the barn renovated. For the ceiling, he commissioned a young, aspiring artist named Tormed Sjaamo, who later went on to become head professor at Oslo's School of Arts and Crafts.

Mountain and sea cultures meet in this Kragerø archipelago barn: there is a model sailboat in the hallway (above) along with an elaborate, colourful old rural shelf (right) which the family moved here from their lodge in the Gudbrandsdalen valley mountains. The barn's exterior is panelled red, contrasting with the dark green round timber interior walls; the decor seems closer to the mountains than to the sea, but boating and swimming are just yards away.

Mr Hans Hopland's new one-room vacation cabin (left) sits hidden among windblown, crooked trees on Jomfruland island. There is no electricity and the well is the only source of fresh water in this bucolic simplicity. It would be difficult to get any 'closer' to nature. On the other hand, summer is quite a different affair in this vast trading house (top) where each spacious room is painted in a different colour.

The barn stands on metre-thick foundation stones and was meant to be a place for social occasions, but it soon became clear that it would make a charming residence. The new generation found it so charming that they established their summer home there, sleeping in the hay loft. The place was furnished with a large old farm table, finely carved and painted 18th-century sideboards, various pieces of lyed furniture and specially made iron lamps to add an extra note of refinement.

THE LITTLE STONE CABIN. Most houses in Norway, even large ones, are made of wood, but Hans Hopland's stone cabin by a beach on Jomfruland (virgin's land) Island east of Kragerø, is an unusual exception. Mr Hopland used to spend his summer holidays sailing and did not want more things in his summer house than he would normally have on a sailing boat. He commissioned architect Arne Gjøen to fulfil his dream.

This unconventional Sørlandet house is set on a seven kilometre-long narrow island of boulders, gravel and sand—the moraine of the southern coast of the Oslofjorden. Here, Mr Hopland leads a kind of Robinson Crusoe existence. His cabin is a low, single-storey structure made out of the same materials as the island itself and almost invisible. Its interior consists of a single room, which has the advantage of needing just five minutes to be swept clean at the end of the season. The furniture consists of made-to-measure benches which convert to beds at night. In the morning, Mr Hopland and his son, Eirik, only have fifty metres of pebbled beach to cross before enjoying their first swim of the day. Autumn and winter storms ensure that plenty of driftwood is available in summer and Mr Hopland does all his cooking on the stone terrace outside. He draws his water from a well which also doubles as a refrigerator in which he keeps his wine and beer ice cold in a sailcloth bucket.

THE BIG HOUSE ON THE FJORD. In the more hilly fjord landscape of south-west Norway lies a huge old trading house with stables and a bakery. It was bought nine years ago by a family which works in the medical profession. The nucleus of the house dates back to the 18th century, while the rest was built about a century later. For the first five or six years after they bought the property, the owners did most of the renovation on the 350 square metres of living space themselves during holidays and weekends. The renovation has involved a lot of what they call 'architectural archaeology' in order to recover the original construction and decor and restore the strong, traditional local colours.

For the owners, restoring the old house provides a perfect way to unwind from professional life. They take great satisfaction from uncovering the original 18th-century paintwork, which was green in one room and Hardanger red in another, and making the most out of second-hand materials and furnishings. The rooms are furnished with light birch-wood Empire and Biedermeier tables, chairs, desks and chests of drawers. There are 17th-century Polish prints and there is even an old house organ. To complement the building's Empire architecture, the owners found traditional Danish, Swedish and Norwegian striped and chequered textiles for the curtains, draperies and seat covers.

Lots of fresh berries and homemade bread (they will be able to bake even more once the oven in the little red bakery has been restored) is always available. There is also the garden to attend to with its old rosarium and centenary perennials. While the tourists pass by on the road that leads up from the local ferry pier, the owners, with so much to

With one living room painted in red and another in green, the family chose to paint the third a strong cobalt blue, furnishing it with an inherited house organ (left). They are quite proud to have furnished this cheerful kitchen with used furniture (right). For many Norwegians, restoring their homes themselves is a favourite way of escaping the strains of modern professions. Picking succulent red cherries from the garden (above) is one of summer's pleasures in this fjordside tradehouse.

keep them occupied, rarely leave home. They cannot imagine a more delightful place to spend the warm summers.

THE HOUSE WITH A HISTORIC PAST. Summer temperatures in northern Norway tend to remain a few degrees lower than in the Sørlandet, 2000 kilometres away, and the sea definitely feels colder. The northern regions are not without their hot spells, however, and summer is at its most dramatically beautiful among the fjords and islands of Nordland, Troms, Finnmark and on the Laplanders' inland plateaus.

Before coming north, it is best to put all the well-worn clichés about the Midnight Sun out of your mind, because none of them do justice to it. One of the most exciting ways to experience the Midnight Sun is on the deck of a ship heading north, at night, up the Raftsundet Sound past the Lofoten Islands. At the top of the sound the land closes in on either side and the channel becomes so narrow that you can almost reach out and touch the cliffs on either side. Then suddenly, the cliffs slide apart, and the sun hits you straight in the face as you come out into an unbelievably beautiful scene of small grey islands stretching out before you on the calm, glittering sea. For people who live north of the Arctic Circle, that imaginary line twenty-three degrees from the North Pole, such extraordinary sights are part of everyday life. It is no wonder that life explodes in the northern regions after the dark winter months.

Astronomical theories start to take on a concrete reality in the north. This close to the pole, conditions gradually go from one extreme to the other as the year progresses. The same could be said of the people as well. Even north of the Arctic Circle, whose position, according to the experts, corresponds in summer to the Earth's angle in relation to the sun, the phenomenon of the Midnight Sun does not start at the same time everywhere. The further north you go, the earlier in the year it starts. On Spitsbergen, at seventy degrees, Norway's northernmost island, the sun remains constantly above the horizon as early as 19th April and starts to go down only on 23rd August. At the North Cape, the northernmost tip of mainland Norway, the Midnight Sun lasts from 12th May until 1st August. Further south still, Svolvær fishing port in the Lofoten Islands can only boast of Midnight Sun between 25th May and 18th July.

At Skånland, the property owned by Anne Margrete Lilienskiold Mehren and Haakon Mehren on the ragged, mountainous coast by Saltfjorden, south of Bodø, the summer light becomes intense from 1st May. "The light is so bright at this time of year that from Skånland we can see all the way out to the Lofoten Islands fifty or sixty kilometres

Up in the Great North, you find turfed roofs not only on wooden farmhouses but on elegant manors as well, like the legendary 1792 Skånland in Salten (top). This elegant manor house has twenty rooms and a fine pilaster dining room furnished with baroque and rococo pieces, but the rustic *Bondestuen* (Farmers' room) (above) serves as the Mehren family's everyday summer living room. Smoked ham and cured leg of lamb hang from the beams, but fish has always been the staple food because of the strong fishing traditions of the Nordland county coast (right).

away," explains Mr Mehren, a privateer who divides his time between Skånland, Oslo, and Spain.

Mrs Mehren comes from this part of the country and she acquired Skånland in 1967 from the Schjelderups, an old trade and shipping family whose prominent role in Arctic life goes back to the 17th century. Skånland was the heart of the Schjelderup's prosperous little empire, with its legendary polar vessels. In 1928, it was Ludolf Schjelderup who, from the crow's-nest of his ship the *Quest*, spotted the Arctic expedition led by Italian explorer Umberto Nobile. Nobile had set out for the North Pole in an airship, but had run into difficulties. In 1936, the Frenchman, Count Gaston Michard, owner of part of the Suez Canal, sought refuge at Skånland when he feared that war was about to break out in Europe. Although the locals were used to rich foreign eccentrics, the count made quite an impression by refusing to walk and

This proud old Kjerringøy trading station situated by the wild, wide Vestfjorden between the Lofoten archipelago and the mainland, incarnates all the magic of the Great North. The yellow and red buildings (right and below left) of its commercial and industrial courtyard present themselves with naked elegance on the ragged northern shores, so extraordinary during the white nights of the Midnight Sun. In areas where neither tile nor slate existed, turf roofs were quite ingenious since the turf helped to isolate the house and was held in place with the *torvvol* (wooden plank). Birch bark served as a rainwater gutter (above).

insisting on being carried everywhere. He returned to his chateau three years after fleeing France only to find himself trapped in a country at war a few months later.

Today, Skånland, with its piers, moorings, boathouses and shops dating from the old trading days, is run as a modern agricultural enterprise, with cows, oxen and horses. A protected 750-acre pine forest is reputed to be the finest in Norway. The main house is thirty metres wide and has a grass roof. Inside, the original baroque and rococo interior is still intact. Mrs Mehren spends most of the year at Skånland and occasionally receives a visit from Queen Sonja, back from a hiking trip in the nearby Salten mountains.

AN OLD TRADING POST BY THE VESTFJORDEN. One of the most famous trading centres in northern Norway is Kjerringøy (woman's island), named, according to legend, after the widow who owned it in the 16th century. Kjerringøy consists of some fifteen white, yellow or red buildings and lies on the mainland coast by the Vestfjorden (western fjord). With its rich history, beautiful buildings and scenic surroundings, Kjerringøy has come to symbolize the magic of the Great North. It is now a museum village run by the Nordland county museum in Bodø, the regional centre.

Strategically located on the north coast trading route by the stormy Vestfjorden, Kjerringøy was an important trading post. Fishermen used to come here to sell their catches to the Kjerringøy merchant who then sold them to the merchants in Bergen further south, from whose shops the fishermen bought their supplies. That made the Kjerringøy merchant a powerful person in the region, and the size of the trading post reflects his status. He was like a monarch ruling over everybody, loved and feared more than anyone else.

Kjerringøy as it exists today was built in the early 19th century by the Sverdrup family. By the middle of the 19th century it had changed hands and belonged to Erasmus Benedikt Kjerschow Zahl, a legendary figure in his own lifetime and the inspiration for the character of Mr Mack in the novels of Knut Hamsun, 1920 Nobel prizewinner. In his works *Rosa* and *Benoni*, read and loved by Norwegians of all ages, Hamsun paints a vivid picture of life at Kjerringøy, drawing directly on his own experiences of the place. During this phase of Kjerringøy's history, an elaborate trading system was in place and as many as one thousand fishermen could be present at any one time.

The most important buildings at Kjerringøy were painted white. The largest was the owner's house, a big Empire building with large

In his novels describing the great trading station on the northern archipelago, Knut Hamsun described life at Kjerringøy as if he had known it himself: the master's aristocratic white main house with its Empire-inspired rooms (above) and large salon with heavy curtains and late 19th-century furniture (right). About Kjerringøy's master, whom he calls Sirilund, he wrote, "In the same room there was also a book-cabinet, where there were even old French books. Mr Mack was a thinking man."

The eight old farm buildings that painter John Collett Anker has collected to create his strikingly beautiful tenant farm, Vaddaas, are dwarfed by the Telemark landscapes. The smallest house is the 1830s timber shed nestled among the birches and meadow flowers, now the loo (left). Mr Anker bought the 1790 mountain cottage first (above), and lives there during the summer, if he does not choose to sleep in one of the old farm beds in the other timber houses. Artists were often among the first private collectors of these rustic old farm buildings and furniture.

aristocratic rooms overlooking the pier. Only those who were specially invited came to the house. Kjerringøy was a tight, self-contained community in which everything was interrelated, even the colours of the buildings. For example, while the front of the main house is white and the back is yellow ochre to match the buildings around the rear 'garden courtyard'. These yellow buildings provided accommodation for staff, and housed shops, a telegraph, and facilities for fishermen. Some of the shops can still be seen today. Deliveries and shipments were made in the red buildings grouped around the 'industrial courtyard' where hundreds of fishermen were housed during their stay. It is fitting that some of the old trading boats—nordlandssjekter—upon which Kjerringøy's prosperity was based, are now displayed here.

Today, Kjerringøy is open all summer and draws tourists instead of fishermen. It is possible to linger in the main house, with its heavy draperies in the doorways between rooms, its birchwood tables and chairs and the enormous sideboards standing against floral wallpapers. One of these rooms in particular provides a fine example of an Empire interior, decorated with dark blue walls, white wall panels, and gilt-framed portraits of figures from the past. After Mr Zahl's death, all of his furniture was sold at auction, something that would probably have saddened him immensely. Fortunately, the house was later refurnished with furniture from the same era—the mid-19th century—and has been brought back to life again, looking much as it did during its heyday.

You can stay overnight at Kjerringøy, but do not expect to be able to sleep there. The best thing to do is to go for a long walk along the beach under the midnight sun, returning for a morning cup of coffee on the old pier in front of the house. On such nights you have the feeling that summer will never end.

Farmhouses in Telemark. Despite the undisputed attractions of summer by the coast, some Norwegians insist that the best place to spend the season is inland, surrounded by the forests, lakes and mountains where the heat vibrates in the clover meadows of the valleys.

For most of the year, John Collett Anker, a painter and descendant of two of Norway's most illustrious aristocratic families, gets all the sun he could wish for on his little farm in southern Spain, with its orange, lemon and fig trees. But when summer arrives and the heat becomes too intense, he follows the migrating birds back north to his old farmhouses on a hillside in Flatdal, Telemark. The landscape here has become famous due to the work of generations of Norwegian artists and Mr Anker usually spends the summer days outdoors painting landscapes in the grandiose scenery of a nearby valley, while drifting clouds continuously change the colouring of the dark, forest-covered mountains. When the sun sets over the rolling hills, he drives his car back up the little dirt road to his weathered, dark brown timber houses grouped around the steep, grassy farmyard.

This eight-house cluster is so charming that motorists passing on the narrow, hilly road below often slow down for a look. Those who visit this summer home, in an area known for its strong arts and crafts tradition, can admire the simple, rustic beauty and elegance of the houses that Mr Anker has been collecting over the years. It has been more than forty years since he moved his first old timber building, a house dating from 1790, to this grassy hillside from its location five kilometres away. The main house has two minuscule rooms with low doorways and worn, red floors. The old tables and chairs and the canopy bed by the fire are

Mr Anker has installed his painter's studio in the old barn. Birch seedlings take root in the turf roof that must be cut every two years (above). He usually paints outside in the neigbouring valleys right in the heart of a vast, breathtaking landscape that contrasts with the closed-in spaces of the main house: the living room (left) with its large fireplace for chilly days, the kitchen, the bedroom behind it, and a sleeping space beneath the eaves and up the steep ladder. Wooden walls were made solid in those days, and the wide red, plank floor has aged well and acquired an attractive patina. The chair by the ladder is from the Danish Baltic island Bornholm. In the small simple kitchen (right), a 14th- or 15th-century hearth house dresser stands at a handy distance from the little folding table.

painted delicate colours and have a rustic charm. The narrow, low-ceilinged kitchen contains a dark, wooden, 14th- or 15th-century hearthhouse sideboard in which everything is stored within reach of the old table where Mr Anker has his dinner. Valuable 18th-century Nøstetangen glass carafes, antique Rouen and Delft plates and Spanish and Moroccan pottery are displayed on the window sills and shelves in the sitting room. They form a refined collection that represents both the local rural traditions and the owner's international tastes.

Mr Anker's houses look so natural on the hill that you would think they had always been there. In fact, this supposedly typical rural home has been put together over a period of years, with buildings gathered from various valleys in Telemark: an old mill from a neighbouring valley serves as a sauna and shower; a tiny, weathered, 1830s wooden hut with a superb view of the mountains is used as a toilet; the barn, with its grass roof, is Mr Anker's studio and contains a fine old farm bed in case one of his guests stays overnight. Another building, which dates from 1802 and comes originally from a valley in the Hallingdal further north, provides an extra bedroom in windowless darkness, while in the *stabbur*, where sausages used to be hung, a superb little guest room has been created with a luxurious antique built-in bed, and lavish, painted decorations. A total of ten beds are scattered among Mr Anker's various houses. Behind the houses, whose grass roofs need to be cut every other year, lies a track used by the neighbour's sheep. Small bells around the sheep's necks announce their approach as they make their way to and from the summer pastures.

PAINTED BEDS IN AN OLD PRESBYTERY. In Flatdal, Mr Anker lives among a circle of friends who share his interest in Telemark's rich artistic heritage. Just down the sharply winding road, in a landscape immortalized by such Norwegian painters as Thorvald Erichsen, Henrik Sørensen, Kai Fjell and Harald Kihle, stands the old Nutheim inn, renovated by painter Erlend Grøstad who now runs a summer painting school there. Twenty-two years ago, Mr and Mrs Grøstad enriched their property by transferring an early 16th-century two-storey timber house there that used to belong to the parish priest. Mr Grøstad acquired it twenty years ago and moved it from its location some kilometres away to a small grove close to the inn.

The grand upstairs bedroom in the house has been furnished with exceptional old farm furniture, and the luckiest of the Grøstads' students get to sleep in what are possibly Norway's finest antique beds. Two towering canopy beds occupy the large bedroom with a curving,

On sculptors' Ellen Grøstad Barstad and Trygve Barstad's old tenant farm, Blengsdalen, in Telemark, Mr. Barstad's angel sculpture flies high on an outbuilding wall (above). Woodworking is one of the important folk art traditions which are especially strong in this part of the country. During the last century, many of Norway's greatest painters, including Thorvald Erichsen and Henrik Sørensen, came to this region, enchanted with its magically sombre blue-green rolling forests and hills. Today, students at painter Erlend Grøstad's summer art school often gather in the intimate kitchen (right) of his 16th century parish priest house.

red dresser decorated with lush paintings of army officers, trees, and houses. The beds were painted in the early 19th century by the renowned local painter Thomas Luraas, for a farm in a neighbouring valley. When the owner wanted to get rid of them, Mr Grøstad and his friend Mr Anker enthusiastically brought them to Flatdal.

Mr Grøstad's daughter Ellen, and her husband, Trygve Barstad, are both young sculptors who live nearby. They returned from Oslo's art milieu in the 1980s to settle in Flatdal's hills where they and their children reside in a nearly two-hundred-year-old tenant farm. When they bought it, the farm was considered to be almost beyond saving, but after years of hard work, little money, and much furniture-making themselves, they succeeded in creating a welcoming home surrounded by lush green forests and meadows. They both work in the sculptor's studio in a barn across the yard, and help each other at critical stages of the artistic process. Some of their sculptures never leave the farm. One of these is Mr Barstad's striking bronze sculpture of a heavily pregnant woman high up on the outside wall of the barn.

A ROCOCO TIMBER FARM. For Mrs Tone Bratland, it is not unusual that tourists stop their cars when passing through the courtyard of her beautiful farm, Hylland Nordigard (northern town). Located in Vinje, further to the west in Telemark, Hylland Nordigard is an exceptional timber farm, famous for its carved galleries and 14th-15th century *ivistoga* (upper room), one of the finest in the country. The *ivistoga's* wooden wall panels are covered in magnificent rococo decorations depicting the sufferings of Christ. They were painted in the late 18th century in delicate, refined blues by the renowned Telemark artist, Aslak Nestestog. Nestestog was twenty-nine at the time and is said to have had a love affair with the mistress of the farm before her marriage to the Hylland farmer. Nestestog painted her portrait on the sideboard which is sandwiched between two wild-looking men painted on the wall on either side. In addition to wall paintings, the *ivistoga* also has white, flower-decorated corniches on the beamed ceilings, and contains a large, blue canopy bed, a big farm table, and various other exceptional, colourful pieces of farm furniture which have been acquired through the generations.

Like many Telemark farms, Hylland Nordigard, with its eighteen acres of cultivable land and its mountain pastures, cannot sustain a family these days, so the Bratlands, like many farmers, also have a shop and a chalet business.

Mrs Bratland was born on the farm and likes to keep alive the family

In Telemark county's Vinje area, contemporary authors Tarjei Vesaas and his wife, Halldis Moren Vesaas, combine writing with life on their farm, Midtbø. A more exceptional Vinje interior is hard to find than at nearby Hylland-Nordigard farm, decorated with famed rural artist Aslak Nestestog's 1787 rococo wallpanel paintings of Christ's sufferings, and a fine box bed (left). Great 20th-century painters like Henrik Sørensen and Reidar Aulie have been guests at this farm with its 1742 loft, or two-story *stabbur* (top and above).

traditions, like sewing and embroidery. Her national costume, worn for festivities and funerals, is the West Telemark blue woollen *bunad*. With its traditional rich, red and white embroidered scroll designs and elaborate silver brooch, this is regarded as Norway's most beautiful *bunad*, and, not surprisingly, takes three months to finish.

Sᴜᴍᴍᴇʀ ʟɪꜰᴇ ɪɴ ᴏꜱʟᴏ. July is the month when most Norwegians rush off to their holiday destinations, but some prefer to enjoy summer life at home. Many people who live in Oslo choose to stay in the capital or close to it, and when you fly into the city, you can appreciate its extraordinary summer setting, idyllically located at the end of the broad, light Oslofjorden (Oslo fjord). With islands and beaches just a short drive from the centre, there is no shortage of contented bathers, sunbathers, and boat users in and around Oslo.

In the past, well-off Osloers had summer homes a comfortably short distance from town. Wives and children would spend the entire summer there, while the men shuttled back and forth from work on weekends. Times have changed, of course, and women also have busy professional lives now. Oslo, like other Norwegian towns, has expanded. The old summer houses in this picturesque landscape of islands and peninsulas are now mostly permanent homes. Most have been built a stone's throw from the fjord and are connected to the mainland by bridge. Some of them are only accessible by boat, however, and have therefore kept their holiday home status.

If you are looking for a seaside atmosphere, you need not leave Oslo at all. Just walk down to Aker Brygge in the heart of the business district where you can have a meal in the sun on one of the moored restaurant boats with sea birds wheeling overhead. For more elaborate cuisine, you can go to D/S Louise, a red brick seafood restaurant where they serve, among other things, boiled salmon with butter and cucumber salad, wolffish steamed in white wine, and grilled, marinated salmon. Across the street stands the former railway station, the Vestbanen, or western line, built in 1872, with its yellow brickwork and twin towers. The building is now used by the National Organization for Arts and Crafts who carefully select craft items from all over Norway for display. Here you can let your fantasies run free among the displays of contemporary ceramics and handblown glass, handwoven textiles, and unorthodox knitwear.

Aɴ ɪꜱʟᴀɴᴅ ʜᴏᴍᴇ ɴᴇᴀʀ ᴛʜᴇ ᴄɪᴛʏ. "When you have a summer home so close to Oslo, it is easy to come into town to work and see friends."

Novelist Knut Faldbakken (top), whose books have been translated into seventeen languages, keeps in close touch with Oslo's changing social climate by (among other things) lunching at D/S Louise where old ship-chests are fixed to the ceiling (above). The restaurant is located at Aker Brygge, Oslo's new seaside center, which bustles in summer. In the middle of the canal stands sculptor Marit Wiklund's 1989 "Utferdstrang" ("Urge to get out in the world") (right).

Many of Oslo's old summer family villas have been turned into year-round homes. The Lampes' villa, however, on an island within minutes of Oslo, is inhabited only as of early May. The decor is casually elegant, with a horsehair-covered Biedermeier sofa (left) and a table with a glassed-in old engraving. The small 18th-century German urn is made of wood and plaster. Mr Lampe, an architect, personally designed the restroom tower (top) and arranged many of the charming kitchen details (above).

says Hans Parr Lampe. This architect and his family spend the summer in an old wooden villa on an island on the western outskirts of Oslo. In their small boat, with its 10 hp engine, they can be in the centre of Oslo in fifteen minutes. The property extends over three acres and has one of the best natural harbours in the area, sheltered from all but west winds.

From mid-May until late September, Mr Lampe, his potter wife Marian Heyerdahl—daughter of the distinguished explorer Thor Heyerdahl—and their daughter, Elisabeth, make the island their home. The villa's small, intimate rooms are painted yellow and white and feature French Quimper faience and examples of Mrs Heyerdahl's own work. The rooms are furnished with urban antiques, two of the most striking of which are an elegant, horsehair-covered mahogany, Biedermeier sofa and a model of an old sailing ship in a glass case.

The house was built in the 1890s and was bought by Mr Lampe's grandfather before the Second World War. During the war, the family kept a cow here until it fell through the boathouse roof one day. The Lampe-Heyerdahls drive a 1952 Citroen on the mainland and are not easily seduced by modern fads. Here, they lead a privileged summer life whose typical daily schedule may include a morning dip, a set of tennis on the clay court or a round of bowls on the lawn, lazing on the veranda and a sail in their small wooden sailing boat, Marusjka.

A HOUSE BY ARNE KORSMO. Textile designer and watercolourist Brit Sæther Johannessen and her artist husband Jens Johannessen spend their summers even closer to Oslo. During the year, the family divides its time between the Oslo area, in a delightful old mountain chalet in the Hallingdal, and a house near Biarritz in France. When the warm days arrive, their white villa near Oslo, built in 1937 on a lush tree-scattered peninsula, turns into a vast, luxurious summer house. They have everything they need here to enjoy the season to the fullest. A steep path leads down from the clean-lined, concrete house through the trees to their own private beach. On the wide slate terrace they enjoy the view over the glittering sea from the comfort of Le Corbusier furniture.

The one-and-a-half acre garden is something of a luxury this close to Oslo. Summer arrives a month earlier here by the water than it does in the Holmenkollen hills surrounding the city, and the garden is redolent with summer fragrances of lavender, honeysuckle and rhododendron plants. There are also wild strawberries and oak and pine trees.

The house, with its spacious rooms looking over the sea, was designed by Norway's internationally acclaimed functionalist architect, Arne

Mr Erling Neby's Oslo home is situated right next to Vigeland Park. Not surprisingly, Mr Neby has chosen to play up the contrast between the lush greenery of the park and the contemporary design of the rooms that lead to the swimming pool (left). The painting in the dining room is by Norwegian New Yorker Jan Groth, a personal friend (below).

Renowned functionalist architect Arne Korsmo designed this elegant white year-round villa in 1937 (bottom) close to the centre of Oslo. Owner Brit Sëther Johannessen created the blue sculpture as a pendant to the "Korsmo blue" door.

Korsmo, who designed Norway's prize-winning pavilion at the 1954 Milan Triennale. Mrs Johannessen's businessman father and her mother, an architect who was a student at the Bauhaus, not only commissioned Korsmo to design the house but the furniture and silverware as well. Mrs Johannessen was brought up in the house and has used her skills to design an additional wing that contains an exceptionally light studio with a loom, and a fireplace, which also provides an extra room for family and friends.

This is a highly design-conscious house. The furniture by Korsmo, Mies van der Rohe, Alvar Aalto, Le Corbusier and Bruno Mathsson stands on bare wooden floors. It is not exclusively modern, however, because there are some antique chairs from the Hallingdal and an exquisite 1706 Numedal painted armoire which stands on the black slate floor downstairs in the airy, open entrance hall. Paintings by the Johannessens as well as works by other 20th-century artists such as Johs Rian, Kai Fjell (her mother's cousin), Aage Storstein and Olivier Debré hand on the walls. The doors of the house are painted a strong 'Korsmo' blue. The large windows are ideal for watching the sun set in the huge western sky.

In summer, there is plenty for the couple to do. They can relax on the terrace, go bathing off the wooden pier by the pebbled beach, take the motor boat out to the islands for the day, or potter about in the garden. Everyday life is kept simple and they have little outside help with the property. An experienced, inventive cook, Mrs Johannessen unwinds by preparing lots of delicious fresh fish and vegetables in her spare, functionalist kitchen.

A VILLA BY VIGELAND PARK. When summer arrives and Erling Neby throws open the terrace doors of his white villa, the capital's most impressive lawns lay before him. These apparently endless lawns are actually part of Oslo's Vigeland Park, the site for a collection of massive nudes by sculptor Gustav Vigeland. The park is silent in winter, reduced to graphic simplicity by the snow. In summer, it comes to life.

A music electronics businessman in his forties, Mr Neby collects art of a different kind, from the granite and bronze figures and 'circles of life' in the nearby park to an abstract yellow steel sculpture over the terrace. From the exterior, the villa, built during the First World War, seems like a traditional, two-storey building with a black tile mansard roof. When he acquired the house in 1976, however, Mr Neby commissioned architect Tore Kleven to redesign the interior. All the internal walls on the ground floor were removed to create one large living space, ideal for exhibiting his impressive collection of huge contemporary canvases. Mr Neby, a dark-haired, boyish, restlessly enthusiastic man, started collecting when he visited the gallery of Denise René in Paris in 1970. His first purchases were works by Jean Dewasne and Vasarely. Later, he bought works by Josef Albers, Olle Baertling, Paul Osipow, and Thornton Willis. Among the most striking works though, are those by Norwegian New Yorker Jan Groth—huge black canvases and tapestries with flashes of light—and the monumental black works by Bjørn Ransve. Mr Neby willingly lends his artwork to galleries when requested and his collection was recently shown at Oslo's Museum of Contemporary Art.

Mr Neby's taste for the modern extends to his furniture, which includes pieces by Mies van der Rohe, Bertoia, Shiro Kuramata, Gae Aulenti, Charles Eames, and Eero Saarinen. Ever since he discovered Knoll in Paris as a nineteen-year-old, and bought his first Mies van der Rohe chair, he has loved modern furniture. In order to add an extra dimension to the room, Mr Neby likes to play jazz and opera music at loud volumes through his huge black loudspeakers. He feels there is much more to Norwegian music than Edvard Grieg and listens to the works of contemporary composers such as Fartein Valen and Finn Mortensen, as well as the electronic music of Arne Nordheim.

So, from June until August, this is how Norwegians live their idyllic summers. It is a time when nobody is quite sure where the days end and the nights begin, a time when all that matters is the sun and the gentle breeze, our swims in the sea and our treks up the baked mountain trails. Then, one day, we notice that the sea feels just a bit cooler and that the sun is lightly veiled, and we realize that summer is not endless after all. Time starts again as the season begins to change.

In the heat of summer, the family takes lunch *al fresco* on the terrace or in the welcome shade under the trees (above) by the path leading from their "Korsmo villa" down to the beach. When darkness falls for a few hours over Oslo's inner fjord, lights are turned on for a late night dinner in the elegant little pier pavillion in (right) Bygdoy's residential area. Lights from Oslo's harbour glitter across the water.

AUTUMN

With their vibrant colours, Norwegian folk art treasures
brighten the farms on the high plateaus, the old
post-houses transformed into hotels, and the farm-museums.
Oslo's season is at its height.

As the precious, sensuous weeks of summer draw to a close, the first unmistakable signs of autumn begin to appear. By mid-August, the sea starts to get colder, the leaves begin to turn red and yellow, and there is a chill in the early morning air. Autumn seems to be drawing us away from the coast where we have been revelling in summer's long, sunny days. There is a growing sense that it is time to put an end to summertime frivolities, to head inland and start preparing for the winter.

After weeks of sun and sea, we shut up our little vacation homes and return to the warmth of our inland and mountain houses. Their tarred, scented, round timber walls, panelled interiors painted in deep, warm, autumnal reds and browns or strong blues and greens, and their reassuringly cosy rooms echo the transformation of nature itself, reminding us that autumn is a time for cocooning indoors.

Crisp dark evenings close in, intensifying the comfort of being inside, and if you prefer to shut the night out, you can draw the curtains and curl up in a big sofa in front of a crackling fire. As the temperature drops, you suddenly feel the need for those snug, woollen sweaters again, or for wrapping yourself in a huge blanket. The rural instinct to store food for the winter is ingrained in the Norwegian character and even those who are firmly anchored in city life fill their freezers with meats, mushrooms, fruits and berries. Pleasant smelling firewood is lined up against the basement wall and inner windows of double glazing are put back in, while in the fields, the combine harvesters work overtime to finish the harvest before the autumn rains and the first sub-zero temperatures.

When autumn comes, Norwegians take long walks in the mountains and forests, like those bordering Raasjoen lake (right), north of Oslo, since this is the season for picking berries and mushrooms. Heather (left) is also in season, and ornates this delicate rose-painted box. The red rowantree fruits (preceding pages) will ferment on the farmer's shelf to become a delicious golden jelly that serves as a perfect accompaniment to game dinners.

RUSTIC ART ON A HALLINGDAL FARM. The 18th-century farm Finnesgard is located in the Hallingdal valley. one of Norway's richest areas for folk art. These twenty-seven dark brown. timber houses stand on a clearing in a hillside forest 760 metres above sea level. Valentin Huitfeldt. still only a law student in his twenties, assumed a heavy responsibility when he inherited Finnesgard in 1989. He combines his studies with managing the property. working in close collaboration with the couple in charge of the day-to-day running of the farm. Finnesgard is a traditional farm with forestry activities. cows pastured in the mountains. pigs. dogs. cats. and a horse called Oscar.

Mr Huitfeldt's great-grandfather. shipowner Rudolf Olsen. bought Finnesgard in 1916 for his hunting trips. He kept the buildings in immaculate condition and the farm was listed in 1923. In the 1940s. it was taken over by Mr Huitfeldt's grandmother who added to the fine

The towering loft (above) is among the twenty-seven exquisite old 18th-and 19th-century buildings on Finnesgard which, like the king's domain in old Norwegian fairytales, stands in a clearing in the spruce forest on the hillsides of Hallingdal valley. The main house (left), built in 1916-18 to provide modern comforts, dominates the outbuildings where farm activities are an ongoing part of Finnesgard's life. When an Oslo shipping family bought Finnesgard, no road led up to the farm, and everything had to be carried up by the workers themselves or on horseback. The rococo sofa (right) below the lead glass windows of the main house is one of the fine rural antiques collected by the owners to furnish their splendid farm.

The painting of German Emperor William (above) is part of the exquisite decoration which Herbrand Sata (1753-1830), the best of the first Hallingdal rose-painters, painted directly onto the panels of one of Finnesgard's early buildings. The panels were later moved to decorate the dining room in the farm's main house (left). A priest can be seen behind the dining room table and, although this photo does not show him, the Czar of Russia is depicted on another panel. Mr. Sata, from nearby Ål in Hallingdal, is regarded as the founder of the Halling style of rose-painting. In his early years, his designs included rococo rocailles and flowers, but later were more baroque. Herbrand Sata's personal development charts the rise of rose-painting in this rich folk art valley.

collection of farm antiques. Some of her additions included furniture originally belonging to Finnesgard, which she managed to recover. Finnesgard's *gamlestuen* (old hall) feels like a small museum. The wall decorations depicting the expulsion from paradise were painted by Herbrand Sata in 1791 and added to the rose-painted charms of the house later by his son, Nils Bæra. The doors are exquisitely painted, with luminous blue marbling on the frames.

Although there is a lot to do during his stays, Mr Huitfeldt rarely misses visits to a log cabin sauna whose 18th-century green, curved glass windows shield him from inquisitive eyes. There has been no hunting at Finnesgard for thirty years now, but Mr Huitfeldt is considering reviving the farm's tradition of grouse hunting as there are lots of wood grouse and a number of white grouse on the estate, in addition to a tribe of elk.

A MAGNIFICENT OLD GUDBRANDSDALEN FARM. Other owners of important rural houses take their responsibilities equally seriously, even if they live outside the country for most of the year. For more than fifty years now, Mr Kjell Holm, consul and businessman, has had one foot in Norway and one foot abroad. Every June, he leaves his Zürich home to return to his magnificent 250-year-old listed timber farm Gamlegarden på Sandbu (the old farm at Sandbu), in the Vågå area off the broad Gudbrandsdalen valley which links central southern Norway with Trøndelag county and Trondheim, the medieval seat of Norwegian kings. The dry, inland climate of the Gudbrandsdalen valley helps preserve the old timber, and the area contains some of the finest old rural houses in the country. Darkened from centuries of harsh weather and sun, these proud, traditional buildings dominate the gently sloping hillsides.

Sandbu, with its twenty-six houses and chapel, is probably the finest among Norway's old timber farms. Originally, it was a medieval farm which was linked with some colourful popular legends; written mention is made of it in the 15th century. The property is also featured in the epic trilogy *Kristin Lavransdatter* by the 1928 Nobel prizewinning author, Sigrid Undset. It was bought early this century by Oslo shipowner Fred Olsen, who later sold it to Mr Holm, upon whom it makes considerable pratical and financial demands. Fortunately, he has the means to keep this vast property in immaculate condition. Sandbu contains richly decorated interiors with glowing round timber walls and galleries and fine old wooden floors. The most outstanding pieces of furniture, a mixture of painted and unpainted rococo and

Rose-painting skills were often handed down from generation to generation; the son served as an assistant in his early years, and father and son often travelled together from farm to farm. Decorating the Gamlestuen (Old House) at Finnesgard was a family enterprise. Mr Herbrand Sata's son Nils Bëra, a fine rosepainter, worked here. Nils is thought to have decorated one room (above) of the Gamlestuen, with its lush blue walls and bold red and white bed, beside the long-legged wooden chest, which could be locked to hold the farmer's money and other valuables. Herbrand Sata himself undertook the decoration of the main room (right) in 1791, when the house was already quite old. He covered one wall with his *The Expulsion from Paradise* and added subtle blue and red decorative elements to the room. An impressive 1892 bridal chest filled with linens and dowry sits in the hallway.

Sandbu's farms (left) date from the late 17th and early 18th centuries and often serve to lodge Mr Holm's visiting friends. Sandbu, in the long Gudbrandsdalen valley, is probably the finest of all the renowned old timber farms around Norway. Rustic and simple on the outside, they hide the richest treasures: fine old farm tables and dressers, cupboards, beds and accessories, some from as early as the Middle Ages. The huge stuffed bear (right), one of the last to be shot in nearby Hedalen valley, guards the gallery outside what used to be the old stable, now furnished with exquisite farm antiques. A simple chair lets one enjoy the view from the gallery (below).

rustic, are the huge canopy beds and painted cupboards in delicious 18th-century colours.

"The upkeep is absolutely colossal," explains Mr Holm. "Every year there is restoration work to see to on one building or another. I work myself into the ground trying to keep Sandbu the way it should be. It does not help matters that I am so damn particular." Despite the fact that Sandbu demands so much hard work, Mr Holm takes enormous pleasure in opening up the old, porticoed houses and putting the furniture, silver, glassware, textiles, and wooden accessories back in their places in the large, high-beamed rooms.

By the time autumn arrives, most of the year's renovations have been completed and the atmosphere at Sandbu becomes more relaxed. A steady stream of visitors passes through its wooden gates, friends on their way to and from their mountain retreats or seeking refuge in the farm's medieval atmosphere from the stresses of urban life. Mr Holm is a close friend of leading Norwegian actors and painters and sometimes plays host to the Norwegian royal family. An attentive host, Mr Holm serves his guests dishes such as wild salmon, with warm cloudberries for dessert. Before leaving for Zürich in the autumn, he invites all his friends in the Vågå area for a farewell celebration. But before he can lock Sandbu's doors again, everything must be meticulously stored away for the winter: furniture and textiles are suspended from the ceilings to prevent the mice from helping themselves while the property is empty.

AN OLD MOUNTAIN INN. Not many people are fortunate enough to inherit a traditional farm, but there are other ways of experiencing life in these exquisite old buildings. One possibility is to stay at Røisheim, a listed coach inn on the edge of the wild Bøverdalen valley in the centre of Norway. In the past, Røisheim was popular with Norway's most famous artistic figures—Grieg and Ibsen were both guests, and painters such as Eckersberg, Hans Gude and Gerhard Munthe also stayed there, no doubt drawn by the mountain colours and the invigorating air.

Today, the inn's guests include VIPs, mountain enthusiasts and prominent industrial and financial figures. People return year after year to Røisheim's small timber rooms with their old farm furniture and traditional woven textiles. The inn is so popular that if you want to come at the best time of the year—between late July and early autumn—you

Even Sandbu's wooden cake stand (above) is centuries old. The flat crisp local cake, called *avlete*, is made of cream, flour and salt. The immense hall in the 300 year-old main house (right) rises through two floors all the way up to the sloping eaves. The 1739 iron stove from Egelands Jernverk near Risør on the Sørlandet coast, is useful on cool days when clothes can by dried on the rack in front of the large fireplace. The doors and their solid irons were made at the same time as the house. Exceptional antiques abound here and include these numerous wooden tankards above the door in which homemade beer has been served since the time of the Vikings. Mr Kjell Holm seats his guests in the hall, around two single-log 15th- century farm tables, each measuring six metres long (left). He found these tables at the end of Jostedalen valley by the Jostedalsbreen glacier to the west, just across the north-south water divide, a region known from the earliest Norwegian myths. The little corner cupboard is early Renaissance, while the pewter plates above the window come from Bergen and date from 1750.

18th- and 19th-century angels that Mr Holm has collected in Bavaria fly high on the canopy bed (above) which Mr Holm made by attaching two smaller beds that he sleeps in during his stays at Sandbu. The 250 year-old Folkestua (People's house) was decorated in 1920 by artist Simon Torbjørnsen in collaboration with antique dealer Mr Dørje Haug, with paintings based on the legends, linked to Sandbu, of 13th century knights (left). A 1769 Gudbrandsdalen chest and a red rococo chair which stands in front of it, is part of a whole period set owned by Mr Holm. The twisted pillar added by a former owner is much more recent.

At Røisheim, the splendid two-hundred-year-old farm in the Boverladen valley, the owner's family silver adds a refined note to the antique décor (above). Rosheim attracted great painters in the 1840s: Johan Fredrik Ecksberg and Hans Gude, whose canvases can be seen at the Nasjonalgalleriet in Oslo; and later, composer Edvard Grieg and writers Henrik Ibsen and Arne Garborg. The painter Gerhard Munthe practically became a family member. He had his own room and visited regularly between 1904 and 1928. Today, mountain-loving guests indulge in hearty breakfasts (right), in the main dining room with its farm and Biedermeier furniture, or in the adjoining dark green and red dining room (left) where a voluminous *trau* sits on the table. *Trau* like these were used for preparing or serving food on all the old farms and were either made of birch or spruce, since pine tended to leave an indesirable taste.

have to book a year in advance. And if you forgot to make this year's reservation before you left last year, your only hope is to have your name added to the waiting list.

The inn belonged to the legendary hostess Signe Moland before being purchased in 1985 by Unni Reinschmidt, the daughter of the local police chief, and her husband, Wilfried Reinschmidt, a Swiss chef who has cooked in a number of prestigious hotels in Europe for people like Paul Getty, the Duke of Windsor, Général de Gaulle and the Aga Khan. One food you can enjoy at Røisheim which you definitely do not get in hotels outside Norway is *gamalost* (old cheese)—brown, crisp cheese with a highly distinctive smell. People either love it or hate it, but *gamalost* enthusiasts simply cannot live without it.

The inn offers an unusual additional service—marriage. Indeed, Røisheim weddings are quite fashionable with the urban chic these days. To give the bridal couple complete privacy, the old *stabbur*—the traditional storehouse built on pillars—has been converted into bridal chambers where the bridal couple spend the night before the wedding downstairs, in separate rooms furnished with narrow beds. The wedding ceremony itself is conducted by a local priest in a little timber hut, following which the couple spend their wedding night in the huge canopy bed in the attic.

Røisheim's continuing popularity as an inn has ensured its survival on its original site, but many old farmhouses have only been saved

because they were bought up by enthusiasts who then moved them to new locations and restored them. Increasingly, however, people are trying to make farms economically viable so that the buildings can remain in their original locations. Christian Sulheim is leading a campaign to ensure that old farms continue, as far as possible, as working farms and he runs an organisation for listed farmhouses in the north Gudbrandsdalen valley. Mr Sulheim himself owns Uppigard (upper farm) Sulheim in the Bøverdalen valley, which consists of twenty-five houses, has been in the family since the 14th century, and was listed in the 1920s. Mr Sulheim feels that it is not enough that people simply be surrounded by the vestiges of a rich rural history. In his view, proper conservation depends on being able to make a living out of the farms. One solution for the future might be to combine agriculture and paying guests. It is certain that it would be difficult to find a more welcoming and relaxing place to sleep than in these old farmhouses with their pungent smell of old timber.

FARM MUSEUMS IN THE EAST. Another way of preserving old houses is to convert them into museums. Three of the best known are the Norsk Folkemuseum in Oslo, Lillehammer's Maihaugen, and the Glomdalsmuseet at Elverum in the Østerdalen valley in the east. Atmospheric farmhouses from various areas, with little prospect of surviving in their original locations, have been collected here. Filled

Like all farms in the old days, Uppigard Sulheim has special buildings for each farm activity, and twenty-one of its twenty-five 17th-century timber houses lie along the sloping yard (above), like the large grain-storage house decorated with a reindeer's horn. The Søre Stugu (Southern House) in which the family and their small children live today (left), dates from around 1650. The rose-painting tradition had not yet been born, so the rooms were not decorated until a century later. The large *klebersten* (soapstone) fireplace (right) dates from the 17th century, and fine old massive and relatively immobile log chairs line up in front of the fire.

The delightful Glomdalsmuseet collection includes eighty-seven old farmhouses from all along the rich Østerdalen valley. But the 1670's Synvisstua farmhouse (left), with its splendid 1744 interior wallpaintings, is something special. The small, single-storey timber house originally stood in Os (in the northern end of the valley) and the paintings were probably done by Mr Synvis Jenssen, the son of a settler who had come here to break in the wild terrain. The white panelled ceiling is decorated with flower and leaf motifs, and on the walls, men merrily play the flute or stand in a fertile landscape, surrounded by biblical quotes. The bedrooms are furnished in a refined, functional manner (above).

The 250-year old Hansmostua farmhouse (right), is also part of the Glomdalsmuseet collection in Elverum. The armoire, which has been placed out of reach of the mice and other rodents, is decorated in the blue marble painting typical of Østerdalen's rose-painting tradition.

with typical marbled blue Østerdalen furniture, these museum houses feel as though they are still inhabited; in one room, a pair of braided birch bark slippers under the bed seem to await their owner.

AN OLD LAKESIDE ESTATE. Some of Norway's largest and most prosperous farms are found around the Mjøsa lake, some eighty kilometres north of Oslo. One of the finest is an old family estate on an island in the middle of the lake. In autumns past, Norway's wealthiest families used to go hunting on the estate's extensive lands with its variety of wildlife, but the current owner is not a hunting enthusiast and prefers to describe the estate's deer, elk, pheasants, peacocks, ducks and hares, as well as the family's cats and dogs, or her pleasant encounters with unsuspecting deer when she is out on her tractor. Her love of animals has obviously been transmitted to her children who have difficulty eating lamb because they cannot forget that the meat was part of a cute animal which they used to cuddle.

The first member of the family came to the farm in 1723. Today, 250 years later, three generations live at the estate. The house, a classical, white, one-storey building with a central tower and a courtyard, was built to replace the old house which was destroyed by fire in 1937. The interior was decorated in a well researched 18th-century style and the large rooms have been filled with furniture dating from the 16th century onwards, including an exceptional Murano chandelier. Everything, with the exception of some fragments of painted wall canvas, has been acquired since the fire. Some of the furniture has been inherited and some was bought at auction where it was selected with a keen eye for style and an appreciation of history and tradition.

The estate covers 220 acres of farmland and forest, so autumn is a busy time. The fields of cereals and potatoes, irrigated with freshwater from the Mjøsa lake, need to be attended to, the cows must be brought down from their free-range summer pastures in September, and there is livestock to be slaughtered before Christmas. The Mjøsa lake is rich in trout weighing up to fifteen kilos, and *lakesild*, a variety of salmon. "There really is a lot to do both indoors and outdoors on a farm like ours," explains the owner. "In the autumn we have such a short time at our disposal, because of the risk of sub-zero temperatures from the middle of October onwards."

A HUNTING AND FORESTRY LODGE. Winter's approach poses no problem for the Fearnley family in their luxurious lodge by Raasjøen lake.

Life on this large property by lake Mjøsa has been quite aristocratic for generations, even though today's owners have their hands full running the farm. In the "English red" panelled dining room (left), the corner cupboard contains fine 18th-century Nøstetangen glass, while the baroque style chairs are copies of those in one of Norway's oldest stone churches nearby. The manor's large hall (right) displays a period rococo canapé and baroque *gyldenlër* (gilt embossed leather) chairs, a Venetian chandelier and the large painting, by Gerhard Munthe.

The lodge is the headquarters of the Fearnley's vast forestry business and forestry work continues unabated right through the winter. To find Raasjøen, you really have to know where you are going. After leaving the open fields behind and passing through the gate at Aas. the Fearnley's sprawling main farm. you find yourself driving on a narrow. twisting lakeside road through endless stretches of forest aflame with autumnal colours. and past giant stacks of cut timber. Suddenly. just when you are beginning to think that you must be lost. you catch sight of the big. low. dark brown lodge built among the trees by the lake.

The Fearnleys came to Norway from Yorkshire. England. in 1753 and went on to found a highly successful commercial dynasty with interests in forestry. shipping. and industry. However. their exploits were not confined to commercial areas: Thomas Fearnley was a 19th-century painter and a close friend of Turner. Indeed. the Fearnleys' friends and houseguests have included the Swedish and Norwegian royal families and some of the most prominent Scandinavian artists and writers of the early part of this century.

The Fearnleys built their elegant lodge at Raasjoen in 1917. The area had been the centre of their vast forestry operations since the 18th century when the Danish king gave them a concession. Just after the war. Raasjøen lodge was the site of the discreet meeting which led to the creation of the three-nation Scandinavian airline SAS. Today. Thomas Fearnley (the latest in a long line of Thomases) and his family

Towards the end of an autumn day, the sun slips away over the large barn building (left). This barn contains numerous bedrooms for large hunting parties at the Fearnley family's 1917 Raasjøen hunting and pleasure lodge, set in the extensive forests of the Hakadal area north of Oslo. In the central hallway (right), elk-horns and family photos attest to generations of hunting pleasure. For guests who prefer strolling down the lakeside forest roads, walking sticks are at hand (below) in the upstairs hall.

The leisurely rural lifestyle of the large agricultural properties continues up here at the lakeside Raasjøen lodge. A nut-tree rococo table (left) in the central Garden Room downstairs is perfect for writing letters near the Swedish tile stove. After a long day outdoors in the forests, sleep comes easily in one of the many double bedrooms upstairs (right), this one with light carvings and elegant blue marbling paintings by Italian artist Dominico Ertmann, who spent months decorating the entire house. The large downstairs living room is filled with exceptional pieces of rural furniture from the 17th century onwards, as well as antique log and simple farm chairs (below).

play host to people from the most prestigious financial and industrial circles. Their guests particularly appreciate the tranquillity and natural beauty of the location, and the antique interiors of the majestic house.

The Fearnleys' lodge is a hidden treasure. The internal walls feature fine stencilled paintings that an Italian artist spent a year working on. Furnishings include handsomely decorated built-in beds and a farm table bought by Mr Fearnley's grandfather that measures almost five metres long. Trophies from many year's hunting line the walls. After today's hunt, the day's game is sampled around the massive dining table from which the diners enjoy views of the surrounding landscape as night descends. Fishing is another popular recreation at Raasjøen—the Fearnleys have thirty-six trout lakes on their property. The Fearnleys stress, however, that their lodge is more than just a place for hunting and fishing. Mr Fearnley was educated in the Yale

This spacious, high-lofted 1936 lodge at Hovet in Hallingdal was built from timber, not stone. Today's owners were inspired by the area's centuries-old houses in their choice of subdued, fine colours for the large living-room (left). Royal Danish Copenhagen china is displayed on the Empire farm dresser (below) that embellishes the rich red-panelled dinig room. A watercolour by artist Jens Johannessen, inspired by the area's local folk art traditions, is also displayed.

School of Forestry and takes the business side of things very seriously, following assiduously in his ancestors' footsteps.

AN EAGLE'S NEST IN THE MOUNTAINS. Hovet (the sacrifice place), the mountain home of textile designer Brit Sæther Johannessen and her painter husband, Jens Johannessen, is like an eagle's nest high up in the jagged mountain range above the Hallingdal valley, north-west of Oslo. The Johannessen's spacious, delightful house lies just below the timber line, at 900 metres above sea level, and close to the main road linking eastern and western Norway. They already knew the region before buying the 1930s timber house fifteen years ago, having rented a house there for some years. The mountainside on which the house is built is scattered with low, weather-beaten trees and small bushes. From the windows, they can see the impressive snow- and glacier-covered Hallingskarvet mountain range, one of the most famous in Norway, measuring thirty-five kilometres in length and reaching a maximum height of 1,875 metres.

"Hovet is where we go when we want to have silence all around us, when we want to get away from Oslo's city life. Life has an extra dimension here which you only find in the mountains," says Mrs Johannessen. When actor Jeremy Irons was visiting Norway for the Haugesund film festival, he was taken up in a helicopter for a view of the mountains and fjords, and declared enthusiastically, "Norway is Europe's best kept secret." Mrs Johannessen strongly agrees. "The drama and intensity of the landscape are absolutely unique. In the clear autumn light, you can see further than anywhere else. We come to Hovet when we start to feel the pull of the mountains, when the yearning for this special mountain feeling becomes so strong that it is almost physical." She describes how the mountain seems to burn in the exceptionally clear autumn light and talks enthusiastically about the abundant game, although the Johannessens themselves never hunt.

Being a textile designer and watercolourist, Mrs Johannessen finds the natural beauty of the Hallingdal region and its rich rural heritage an inspiration. Walking through the striped front door, past the two grouse hanging from the door frame and into the high-ceilinged living room, you are immediately struck by the Johannessen's acute sense of colour. The round timber walls are painted in the traditional Hallingdal blues, reds, and yellows, and the large rooms are furnished with exceptional 18th- and early 19th-century painted cupboards, shelves, chests, tables and beds from various regions in southern Norway. The main sitting room has subtle light blue walls and a white ceiling. The fireplace where the family gathers is a copy of one that Mrs Johannessen saw at a local folk art museum. On one wall hangs an exquisite 18th-century blue Hallingdal cupboard, while against another wall stands an inviting blue antique bed. The wooden floorboards are partially covered by kilims and blue rag rugs, while in the centre of the room stands an old iron weather vane which was found under a *stabbur*. On the walls above the steep wooden stairs hangs a striking still life arrangement: Mrs Johannessen's collection of colourful tartan and floral Hallingdal traditional costumes includes some antiques and some she has made herself.

Hovet's exquisite old Hallingdal colours and shapes have inspired a number of Jens Johannessen's finest paintings. Its peaceful atmosphere and the natural beauty of the landscape make the house a good place to work. They do a lot of their work in a room painted another delicate shade of blue in which little paper bags of colour powder and a pot full of paintbrushes sit on a superb old Hallingdal shelf. Across the yellow hallway is the log cabin-like, deep-red dining room where the family has its meals. The dining table is decorated with branches of red rowanberry, medieval candlesticks made from wood and iron, and Royal Copenhagen blue and white china. Mrs Johannessen loves cooking and her dinners eloquently testify to the fact. A typical starter might be corned trout with mustard sauce, while the main course often consists of mountain game, such as grouse, accompanied by mushrooms, potatoes and rowanberry jelly with whipped cranberries floating in the sauce. Another favourite is fresh trout from the nearby Sudndalsfjord lake.

A SECLUDED HIKING BASE. Another person who enjoys cooking is Norwegian-born Paris couturier Per Spook. Friends who come to visit him often enjoy his speciality of succulent pork *rôti* with all the trimmings in his peaceful turn-of-the-century holiday home in the Sigdal valley, north-west of Oslo. Whenever he can find time to get away from his *haute couture* business in Paris, Mr Spook flies to Oslo and then drives for a couple of hours up twisting lakeside roads to reach Sigdal.

Mr Spook acquired his peaceful little farm, Fossheim (home by the waterfall), twenty-five years ago and has carefully maintained its intimate, homely atmosphere. Fossheim consists of a house, a red barn house, and across the grassy courtyard, a storehouse with an upstairs guest room. The informal interiors at Fossheim are decorated with a combination of 19th-century birchwood and colourful farm furniture, old embroideries and contemporary paintings. The combined living

For Paris' Per Spook (top), autumn represents the supreme moment of happiness. Long mountain hikes in the hills and mountains of Sigdal and beyond greatly contrast with his demanding professional life in Paris. Like all Norwegians, he has a passion for picking mushrooms and wild berries (above), and the homemade rasberry jams are served with light waffles in the welcoming bright blue kitchen (right).

and dining room are bright and airy with their light blue panelled walls and ceilings and exterior white veranda, and the kitchen is painted a strong, dark blue.

Mr Spook knows where to find the best knitwear in Norway and regularly visits the country for his work. He comes to Sigdal, however, for relaxation and pleasure. Mr Spook's many years in Paris have not diminished his Norwegian instinct for storing up nature's produce before winter arrives. In autumn, he sets off with baskets and containers to collect mushrooms and mountain berries for the elaborate, back-to-nature meals he serves his friends in the intimate, lace-curtained dining room at Fossheim. He delights in the wildlife at Sigdal—the elk, deer, grouse and hares, and the trout and *sik* (freshwater herring).

The Sigdal valley is a gentle landscape of forests and fields, neat attractive mountains and glinting lakes. Beyond the trees in Mr Spook's garden, the waters of the river that gave the house its name wash over the rounded rocks. Mr Spook is a keen hiker and you need long legs and good lungs to keep pace with him up the steep forest paths. "Sigdal means limitless freedom to me. It offers the best things in life—creativity, fantasy, closeness to nature. It is an inexhaustible source of inspiration in my life," he explains.

So when autumn comes to Sigdal, the tall, slender couturier, who wears his trademark cashmeres and linen designs whilst in Paris, pulls on his home-knitted woollen sweater and matching cap, his thick woollen trousers and gum boots, and slings his big rucksack onto his back for setting off into the hills.

S<small>EA CAPTAIN'S ISLAND HOME</small>. This communion with nature is not confined to the land. The sea offers a similar experience. When the crowds of boisterous summer tourists have left the seaside town of Arendål in the Sørlandet, the coast's natural beauty starts to reassert itself again with strong autumn colours and sunlight vibrating across the water and, as night falls, the glittering phosphorescence. Across the sound leading into Arendal harbour lies Merdø Island and its old sea captain's house, Merdøgård.

This 18th-century house has now been turned into a museum run by the museum authority in Aust Agder county, and it contains a wealth of objects testifying to the region's rich past. Merdøgård is a kind of monument to the important trading partnership with England and the Netherlands from the 17th century when Merdø Island was a busy trade, customs and sea pilot's station. The Sørlandet coast was one of Norway's most important shipping regions at the time, and the old

On Merdø island outside Arendal, the façade of a building on the pier (top) is decorated with relics from seaside life. The small sitting room of Merdøgard, furnished with Norwegian and English 18th-century furniture, was the family gathering place (above). In these old seaside houses, however, the real centre of family life was the low-ceilinged kitchen (right), whose pewter, copper and English china is neatly arranged on the shelves.

shipping families have become today's prosperous—and sometimes less prosperous—shipowners.

The house has been kept as it was in the region's heyday—it is almost as if the skipper still lived there and had just stepped outside for a moment. Downstairs, the decor is sober and simple. The green living room is furnished with Norwegian and English furniture brought by a Liverpool bride, and like the kitchen with its large fireplace and pretty displays, was used for daily life. The drawing room is more formal, however, and was reserved for more festive occasions when the captain was at home. Merdøgård's treasure is the upstairs baroque hall which shows how foreign influences marked the region, as they do, in the main hall, where there is an 18th-century canopy bed with *toile de Jouy* curtains, an old Continental screen, English mahogany chairs, Dutch clocks, and dark blue English floral wallpapers.

The formal sitting room at Merdøgård (right), reserved for VIPs and special occasions, is decorated in blue and white English wallpaper dating from 1760, a period when commercial exchange in the North sea was extremely active. The portraits and silhouettes are Danish and Norwegian, and the 1798 map is of Merdø island. Brisk trade brought definite sophisticated foreign influences to Sørlandet's ports. Merdøgård's upstairs hall is dominated by an 18th-century canopy bed (above) draped in Jouy cotton and the remarkable 17th-century painted screen (left), possibly brought home from the Netherlands. The decorations have Greek mythological themes, like Artemis judging the nymph Calypso who had won Jupiter's love and aroused Juno's jealousy. The room displays a dark green beamed ceiling and strong red décor; the dark blue and white wallpapers are from the period.

The interior of Bårdshaug manor, which dates from 1897, was the ancient residence of an industrialist, but has now been transformed into an hotel. It is strongly marked by the Dragon style (top) and the family hunting tradition (above). In Meldal, south of Trondheim, the 1898 forest timber villa Fjellheim is one of Norway's finest examples of the rich Dragon style. Berlin-educated architect Finn Knudsen designed Fjellheim, whose monumental dining room windows are surrounded by characteristic Dragon friezes (left).

BEAUTIFUL EXAMPLES OF DRAGON ARCHITECTURE. Trade and an international perspective also lie behind the formal elegance of Bårdshaug at Orkanger by the Trondheim fjord. Bårdshaug, a sprawling, white, wooden manor built in 1897. Its wooden façade is embellished with a tower, and its magnificent rooms are decorated with antiques from throughout Europe an Africa. It was the home of the Thams family who made their fortune in timber, mining, and railways. This extremely wealthy family had distinguished friends from all over the world and now that Bårdshaug is a hotel, guests can sleep in the same walnut Louis XVI bed once occupied by Sweden's King Oscar II, Belgium's King Leopold, Norway's King Olav, and Monaco's Prince Albert.

The family's industrial empire started when Wilhelm August Thams established the first sawmill. But it was his architect grandson, Christian Thams, who made the most important contribution to the family fortune. Born in 1867 and educated in Zürich, this young Norwegian had made a name for himself in Europe by the age of twenty-three. He designed and built, among other things, the little wooden house that served as the Norwegian pavilion for the 1889 Universal Exhibition in Paris and which Gustave Eiffel bought to use as offices. While in France, Christian Thams began designing pre-fabricated wooden houses that were eventually sold throughout Europe, as well as in Africa, South America and India. He later expanded his family's activities in Norway by building up a thriving fish export business, excavating mines at Meldal, and, in 1908, constructing the country's first electrified railroad line, Thamshavnsbanen (Thams harbour line) in order to link the Meldal mines to the port. Christian Thams became a prominent industrialist and served as a minister for the prince of Monaco and the Belgian consul.

In 1898, Thams had the hunting villa, Fjellheim, built relatively near the family mines in the mountains and forests of Meldal. This huge brown timber villa, which bears a strong stylistic resemblance to the Frognerseteren restaurant in the hills above Oslo, was purchased from the Thams family in 1925 by the family of Elias Anton Cappelen Smith and his wife, Kine who now live here. Mr Cappelen Smith's family has been involved in the iron, steel and building material industries in Trondheim since 1869. Fjellheim was designed in the romantic, nationalistic, Dragon style popular at the time and is the ultimate movable residence, a kind of Thams show house intended to demonstrate the potential of prefabricated housing. During construction, all the timbers were meticulously numbered to facilitate reassembly. After completion, all thirty rooms and 350 square metres were dismantled and reassembled in Meldal thirty kilometres away.

Fjellheim is an impressively large villa with huge stone fireplaces, ceiling beams, and ornate, Dragon-style benches along the walls. The dining room can seat up to thirty people and has a huge fireplace with a crackling fire to take the edge off the chilly autumn air. There is no longer any hunting at Fjellheim, although there is still abundant wildlife. Mr Cappelen Smith says that hare, elk, deer and lynx all make frequent visits to the estate, and that there are even wolves in the region which requires that their sheep, who graze outdoors until mid-October, be fenced in.

FISHING VILLAGES IN THE LOFOTEN ISLANDS. It would be hard to imagine a more striking contrast with the gentle, rolling hills of Meldal than the striking, rugged beauty of the windblown islands off Norway's northern coast. Ragged mountain ranges provide a towering

Fjellheim's high-ceilinged dining room (right), with its towering fireplace of painted *klebersten* (soapstone), was inspired by the great Viking halls, with carved chairs and built-in benches along the round timber walls, brass shield wall chandeliers, and a woven tapestry with old Norwegian mythological motifs. Soapstone is so soft that it permits delicate carving, and the soapstone oven (above) in Fjellheim's great hall is elaborately decorated with Dragon designs. A century later, the great Dragon style, now considered to be an important part of Norway's architectural history, blends new international building trends with the country's past.

During the hunts organized by the Fjellheim family, the men slept in a separate older house that was refurbished and decorated with fine flower paintings in 1927 and 1928 by Professor Johan Meyer of Trondheim's Technical University (left).

Lovers of crisp, ocean-side autumn days come to Lofoten archipelago's fishing villages (left), where pierside sheds (right) remind you of the simplicity of lives here in the old days. Dried cod or *tørrfisk* (below) is all-important in the northern regions, and later becomes succulent *lutefisk*, or lyed fish (bottom) and plays an important role in the lives of these Northern residents.

backdrop to the foaming autumn North Sea where the Lofoten archipelago, composed of a chain of small and large islands, extends roughly parallel to the mainland north of the Arctic Circle. The name comes from *lo*, an old word for lynx, and *foten* meaning 'the foot.' On a map the archipelago does look a bit like an animal's foot sticking out into the open sea. The islands are separated by narrow sounds and cover a total area of 1,200 square kilometres. What is most needed here is not so much feet, as a good solid boat.

The islands are dotted with small, wooden fishing villages nestling against the cliffs in sheltered harbours. Nature can be inhospitable and hard here, making it is almost impossible for the inhabitants to build anything more than the smallest, simplest houses. The winds are so strong that you can be blown to the ground and when the weather is bad, you just have to sit it out.

These days, increasing numbers of city dwellers are drawn to this wild region off the beaten track, for it offers seclusion, clean air, and unpolluted waters. Technological changes in the fishing industry have had a big impact here; large modern trawlers with big freezing capacities have devastated the local fishing industry as well as many villages among the Lofoten Islands and the neighbouring Vesterålen Islands. Tourism therefore provides some precious business, and some owners of old fishing stations now rent out their colourful quayside houses to holiday-makers with a taste for the pleasures of a simple, ecological lifestyle.

Aᴜᴛᴜᴍɴ ɪɴ Oꜱʟᴏ. In Oslo, in the south where the sea is less wild, life starts to return to normal from late August and early September. Autumn is a season of intense activity. There is the Ibsen festival at the Nationaltheatret in September, the Høstutstillingen, Norway's national exhibition of contemporary art, and the Oslo Philharmonic Orchestra's season in the modern Konserthuset (concert house). The Grand Café, located on the ground floor of the Grand Hotel with its good views of Karl Johan Street, and its big rival, the Theatercafeen, do brisk business in this active season of homecoming after a long summer absence.

You are in the heart of Oslo between the parliament building and the Nationaltheatret not far from the Royal Palace at the top of Karl Johan Street. Those with something to celebrate can rent the tower suite at the Grand Hotel and enjoy its impressive views of the city centre. Christian Krohg, the highly respected and widely travelled late

"We recognized him immediately, and as he walked through the hotel lobby to the dining room, he reminded me of a doctor on the way to visit his patients. With careful steps, he went to sit in the most isolated corner of the large restaurant," wrote Lugné-Poe, director of the famous Parisien Theatre de l'Oeuvre in 1894. He was in Oslo to stage two of Ibsen's plays and went to the Grand Café to see the author. Ibsen led such a regulated life that the town could set its clocks by him. Everyday at noon, he made his ritual, grand entrance to the Grand Cafe, shown on Per Krohg's monumental painting (above) which has dominated the cafe since 1932. Ibsen's office (right) is furnished in the bourgeois style of *Hedda Gabler*. A stylish 1886 shop interior (left) on Karl Johan Street, where gloves were sold in Ibsen's days, is now the café Tre Brødre (Three Brothers).

The *Kristiana*, one of the capital's most elegant clubs, evokes Denmark by its name, and Sweden by its Gustavian décor that recreates the atmosphere of an 18th-century patrician residence (above and left). Auctions are occasionally held on Sunday.

19th-century Norwegian painter, admitted that during his stays in Paris, he missed Norway's little capital and its women, and that when sitting in the Café de la Paix, he became nostalgic for the 'Grand.' Krohg was one of the famous regulars at the Grand Café along with Henrik Ibsen, Edvard Munch, and Frits Thaulow, who frequented this meeting place for artists, writers, and composers in the 1880s and 1890s, when Oslo was still named Kristiania after the 17th-century Danish-Norwegian King Christian IV. They and the other well known figures of the period are still there, not at the tables, of course, but up on the wall in the huge mural painted in 1928 by Christian Krohg's son, Per Krohg.

The Ibsen festival has added an exciting new dimension to autumns in Oslo. Ibsen lived abroad for twenty-seven years and never owned a comfortable villa like the one Grieg lived in near Bergen, but for the last fifteen years of his life he did have a large flat in Arbiens Street overlooking the Royal Palace and its park in what was, at the time, a highly desirable part of Oslo. Ibsen was on sufficiently friendly terms with King Oscar II and Queen Sophie to be given a key for the gate to the royal park where he used to take contemplative, solitary walks or sit in the Queen's small, wooden pavilion which still stands nestled among the huge old trees. Arbiens Street has changed since Ibsen's time. After his death, the Norsk Folkemuseum reconstructed the writer's office which is housed in one of its buildings. Thanks to the efforts of actor Knut Wigert, the office is to be restored to its original location on Arbiens Street, bringing Ibsen closer to the people who attend the festival which bears his name.

Despite all the events taking place in Oslo, there are still attractions which lure people to the outskirts of the city. One of them is a picturesque small restaurant called the Værtshuset (the inn) Bærums Verk. The restaurant, owned by Andreas Tandberg, is located in one of a cluster of small, red, 17th-century, one-storey houses which used to be inhabited by the workers at Bærums Verk mill, Norway's oldest iron mill that dates back to 1610. The mill still belongs to the wealthy Løvenskiold family who also own vast areas of forest around Oslo. With its low ceilings and white beams, crackling fireplace, Empire furniture, and old, painted wall panels, Værtshuset's interior matches its back-to-nature menus. You would not be surprised to meet a goat standing on the front steps here where the rural mountain atmosphere is heightened by the waiters' grey, knee-length, leather shorts. The fare proposed by chef Morten Kristiansen features elk, grouse, duck and lamb.

After you have finished your meal, a good place to go to for a warming, late night drink is the Kristiania Club in the city centre. Located in what used to be a well-known art gallery, the new Kristiania Club has already become a kind of institution. A wide, grand, wooden staircase links the two floors of large, bare exhibition halls furnished with light cream-coloured furniture in late 18th-century Gustavian Swedish style, and the atmosphere is one of aristocratic opulence.

Despite Oslo's events and entertainments, as autumn closes in and the evenings get darker, life becomes increasingly centered on the home. People create their own small indoor world, cocooning themselves in their homes to take comfort in the pleasures of food and drink and the company of friends, while outside, the weather deteriorates.

WINTER'S ARRIVAL. Suddenly, autumn turns into winter. The lights of Advent lead us into a seemingly endless darkness until the sun turns again just before Christmas. Even people who are not normally church-goers in this Protestant country come together in the flickering candle-light of the richly decorated, red, blue and green old church interiors. A sense of anticipation marks the approach of Christmas and the New Year, and the arrival of longer days. One of the most beautiful churches in the country is the minuscule old Uvdal stave church whose oldest parts date back to the 12th century. The simple brown exterior belies the sumptuous interior with its 17th- and 18th-century rose-paintings in luxuriant reds and blues, its red altarpiece, and blue and white stencillings.

The year has come full circle. This exquisite little church, illuminated by candles, seems a fitting place to celebrate, for it incarnates all that is fundamentally important to Norwegians—the country's rich folk art tradition, the beautiful use of wood, the dramatic landscape, and the irresistible rhythm of the seasons, drawing us ever onwards.

In autumn, Norwegians love to go on long walks in the berum woods on Oslo's western outskirts. To finish off a long day of hiking, you can stop in at Verthu-set Berums Verk (above), a restaurant providing a cosy atmosphere in its low-ceilinged mid-17th-century house. In the city, during the Ibsen festival, the Grand Café of the Grand Hotel, whose windows look onto Karl Johan street, is full of activity. We can almost imagine that we have returned to the *belle époque* evoked by Per Krohg's famous painting (detail right). This long tableau, where we find the portraits of painters, writers and journalists of the epoch, is a testament to Norway's emergence in 19th-century art and literature. Edvard Munch is seated to the right against the window. The woman in the foreground is Alexandra Thaulow whose husband, Frits Thaulow, was a friend of Gauguin.

Amidst red and blue Renaissance rose-painting in the exquisite Uvdal stave church (following page) in the Numedal valley, Norwegians celebrate Advent and the coming of Christmas and the New Year.

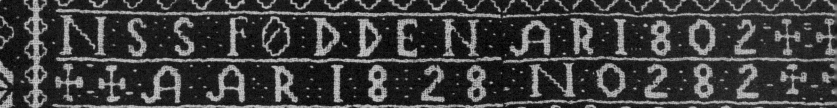

VISITOR'S GUIDE

Where to rent a room in a traditional wooden
house with rose-painting decorations?
How to rent a fisherman's house in the Lofoten
Islands or a "hytte" on the banks of a fjord?
When is the right time to visit Edvard Munch's
home or Henrik Ibsen's study?
Where to buy antique glass, hand-knitted sweaters,
and the very best salmon?
Here are the right addresses in the cities
and countryside of Norway, those which
Norwegians themselves recommend.

These addresses were given to us by Norwegians who guided our approach to their country and opened doors for us in every city. Some of these addresses are well known, others less so. This section not only includes all of the addresses of the hotels, restaurants, cafés and boutiques mentioned or depicted in the previous chapters, but also of other places that we have visited. Norway boasts several very comfortable modern hotels, high-quality restaurants and famous museums which are all listed in tourist guides. We instead chose to emphasize the places with authentic décor and warm atmosphere, the intimate little museums inside the town houses which have kept all of their original charm, as well as those which provide fine examples of Norwegian craftmanship and decorative arts. There is no mention of prices here, but the traveller should realize that Norway is basically an expensive country. To start the day off right, one must enjoy the especially abundant breakfasts served in hotels, that can get the traveller through the day until the early dinner hour (around 4 p.m.). This guide is organized by category. Within each, the order is alphabetic according to the city. Phone in advance to be sure of the hours of service. To telephone to Norway from abroad, ask your local phone operator for the dialling access code. When in Norway, just dial "0" before the numbers listed below. Please note that the following telephone numbers, other than those for Oslo, may be modified due to changes planned for Norway's telephone system. All of the places mentioned below can be found on the maps on pages 220 and 225.

Located on the banks of the Sognefjord and framed by mountains, this is one of the most beautiful wooden hotels still in existence. The lacy ironwork and the terraces with spectacular views of the fjord provide charm, grace, and lightness to this vast 1913 contruction. The hotel is justly famed in the area, and its English-style nobility was highly esteemed at the beginning of the century. Insist on obtaining a room in the older part of the hotel.

Augustin Hotel
C. Sundts Gate 24, Bergen
Tel. 5 230025
One of the rare hotels in Bergen to have held onto the traditional charm of yester-year. A pretty view from rooms looking out on the port.

SAS Royal Hotel
Bryggen, Bergen
Tel. 5 318000
The hotel line SAS, de luxe hotels for business travellers, certainly offers comfort, but is often impersonal. However, the SAS hotel in Bergen is quite remarkable for its architecture, which blends in perfectly with the high-gabled roofs of houses in the port of Bryggen. Once, these houses were sales centres for German merchants from the Hanseatic League. Today they provide one of the loveliest scenes in Norway. The oldest houses date back to the 18th century.

Mundal Hotel
FjÆrland
Tel. 56 93101
Built in 1891, this large inn designed in traditional wooden architecture offers rooms, some with a balcony, with a view of the fjord. It is the ideal spot for a calm, romantic retreat, that is even better if one arrives here by boat. An excellent point of departure for excursions to the surrounding glaciers.

Nutheim Gjestgiveri
Flatdal
Tel. 36 52143
A typical inn in the Telemark Valley, which boasts wooden chalets with sod and grass roofs. In Nutheim, near Seljord, this hotel

offers a pretty view of the whole region. It is a much-appreciated stopover point for visits to Åmotsdalen, the centre of rose-painting.

Elveseter Hotel
Elveseter, Lom
Tel. 612 12000
In a high mountain pasture farm with older buildings dating back to the 17th century, the Elveseter family, farmers and craftsmen, created this rustic but perfectly comfortable country hotel. Not far from the church in Lom, one of Norway's loveliest *stavkirke*, famous for its paintings by Hans Gude, the 19th-century Norwegian master whose other works may be seen in the National Museum.

Røisheim
Lom
Tel. 612 12031
This hotel is comprised of a number of little wooden houses with grass roofs built in the 17th century. The rooms are simply decorated with antique painted furniture. The living room is warmed by a large chimney. In the elegant dining room, traditional menus, changed every day, are served by candlelight. An exceptional

HOTELS

Bryggen Home Hotel
Apotekergate 1-3, Ålesund
Tel. 71 26400
In a former warehouse dating back to the early 18th century, this hotel with a modern interior has pleasant rooms with a view of the sea. It is part of the Home Hotels group, which are generally located in older buildings and guarantee the visitor an intimate atmosphere, a family-style welcome, and constant attention to comfort.

Tyholmen Hotel
Teaterplassen 2, Arennal
Tel. 41 26800
Arendal is one of the "white cities" on the Sørlandet coast. Its port for pleasure-boats is open all summer long. The city's older section is perfectly preserved, with houses made of painted wood, including this long elegant building with modern rooms facing the port.

Kvikne's Hotel
Balestrand
Tel. 56 91101

quality stopover that is much appreciated by Norwegian notables.

Hotel Union
Øye
Tel. 70 62100
This renovated old wooden hotel in the Dragon style still retains turn-of-the-century charm as well as authentic decorations. Famous guests have stayed here, including the Danish novelist Karen Blixen (Isak Dinesen), who chose a fjord in the small town of Berlevåg at the northernmost point of the country, as the setting for her book "Babette's Feast."

Kongsvold Fjeldstue
Oppdal
Tel. 74 20911
Situated right in the heart of Norway, in a natural setting

in the midst of the Oppland mountains north-east of Dombås, this traditional old inn is made up of several houses. Its carefully restored decoration and fine furniture make it an agreeable stopover in a region where one can see herds of reindeer and musk oxen. Also recommended is a visit to the botanical gardens with its exceptional specimens of mountain flora.

Bårdshaug Herregårds
Orkanger
Tel. 74 81055
A fine wooden construction with a lovely decorated

facade in a village to the west of Trondheim. At the beginning of the century, the manor, which is the principal building of the hotel, was a Minister's official residence. Despite the renovation of the rooms, the hotel, which is surrounded by a lovely garden, hasn't lost its charm, nor the decorations of its previous incarnation.

Hotel Ambassadeur
Camilla Colletts vei 15, Oslo
Tel. 22 441835
Built at the end of the previous century, this hotel is renowned as one of the most comfortable in Oslo. Situated just a few minutes away from the city centre in a residential quarter just behind the Royal Palace, its charms are concealed behind a pale pink façade with cast-iron balconies.

Hotel Bristol
Kristian IV's Gate. 7, Oslo
Tel. 22 415840
A famous construction dating from the 1920's, with a pleasant library bar and a grillroom decorated in the manner of a hunting lodge that make this great hotel in the city centre a well-known stopping point.

Hotel Continental
Stortingsgata 24, Oslo
Tel. 22 419060
One of the city's most pleasant hotels; its interiors are decorated with prints by Edvard Munch. The Theatercafeen, a restaurant on the ground floor, is where all of Oslo likes to meet, including actors from the nearby theater. (Liv Ullmann made her theatrical debut there).

Frogner House
Skovveien 8, Oslo
Tel. 22 560056

A very comfortable, charming hotel just recently opened in the heart of Oslo. No restaurant.

Gabelshus Hotel
Gabels Gate. 16, Oslo
Tel. 22 552260
This warm and discreet red-brick hotel, tucked away beneath vegetation, is located at a slight distance from the city centre. It has the charm of a large country house with a perfectly intimate atmosphere. The dining-room looks onto a garden.

Grand Hotel
Karl Johans Gate 31, Oslo
Tel. 22 423330
Edvard Munch wrote that the history of Oslo and that of the Grand Hotel are inseparable. This luxurious hotel always welcomes Nobel Peace Prize winners (which are the only Nobel Prizes awarded in Oslo). It is also the preferred place for official dinners for visiting heads of state. A dream stay is possible in the tower suite, spread out over three floors in the old tower that tops the hotel. There is an unforgettable view of the royal palace, the city, and the Oslo fjord.

Holmenkollen Park Hotel
Kongeveien 26, Oslo
Tel. 22 146090
Located in a park-like setting on a wooded hill near a famous ski jump and only 15 minutes by car from the centre of Oslo, this handsome, red wooden hotel was constructed in 1894 in a style that recalls a Viking ship or one of the famous wooden churches. This hotel is really worth a visit even if you don't plan on staying there. The view of the city and of the Oslo fjord is exceptional.

Walaker Hotel
Solvorn
Tel. 56 84207
For three centuries, the Walaker family has welcomed visitors in this inn comprised of several buildings. Its rustic charm, pleasant garden, and extraordinary setting, on the Sognefjord, not far from the famed Urnes church make this hotel a lovely bucolic stopover.

Stalheim Hotel
Stalheim
Tel. 5 520122
This great hotel with hundred-year-old traditions is quite unique for its setting and spectacular view of three valleys, which can be easily admired from the vast terrace. Located near famous waterfalls, it can be reached via Norway's steepest road. The hotel has its own open air museum comprising about thirty old houses. Reserve in advance because tourists from all over the world want to stay here.

Skagen Brygge Hotell
Skagenkaien 30, Stavanger
Tel. 4 530350
Located in the former buildings of a maritime warehouse on the port, this hotel has modern rooms, brick walls and is decorated with English fabrics. The pleasantest rooms are those with a sea view. Part of the Home Hotels group.

Hotell Lofoten Svolvær
Austnesfjordgt 12, Svolvær
Tel. 88 71999
This charming hotel provides a good base for discovering the Lofoten archipelago. Madame Falk Petersen offers some of the best cuisine in the region.

Bakeriet Home Hotel
Trondheim
Tel. 7 525200
Located in a former turn-of-the-century bakery in the city centre, this charming hotel also offers small apartments for long stays, along with traditional rooms. Part of the Home Hotels chain, in which the visitor is

always welcomed as a privileged guest.

Utne Hotel
Utne
Tel. 54 66983
Founded in 1722 on the banks of the Hardangersfjord, in a region in the south of Voss famed for its fruit trees, this is the oldest hotel in the area. It has been run by the same family for five generations. A set menu is served in the pretty dining-room decorated with traditional painted woodwork. There are only a few rooms, as well as salons with large chimneys which are good for meetings after taking a stroll. This hotel is part of the Romantik Hotel group, all of which are located in antique buildings and which offer their guests friendly service and an intimate atmosphere.

RESTAURANTS

Sjøbua
Brunholmgt 103, Ålesund
Tel. 71 27 100
This restaurant is located in an art nouveau building that is typical of this city. Meals are reasonably priced and the fish is delicious.

Enhjørningen
Enhjørninggården, Bryggen, Bergen
Tel. 5 327919
Found in the old Hanseatic quarter of Bryggen (the docks), this restaurant whose name means "the unicorn" is located in a building dating back to the 17th century. The fish and seafood buffet is impressive.

To Kokker
Bryggen, Bergen
Tel. 5 322816
As its name in Norwegian suggests, two cooks run this restaurant in a building that is over 300 years old. The reindeer meat and fish dishes are particularly tasty here. There is also a *multer* dessert made of arctic raspberries. Its exceptional wine list is quite rare in Norway.

Fiskekrogen
Zachariasbryggen, Fisketorget, Bergen
Tel. 5 317566
Recently opened on the market square, this small, popular restaurant serves fish and game. Its décor is inspired by great sailing ships. Among the specialities is a fish soup that is a meal in itself. It is also the ideal spot for tasting grilled elk or a side of venison.

Ambassadeur
Camilla Collets vei 15, Oslo
Tel. 22 552531
A very good restaurant located in the Hotel Ambassadeur. Light cuisine. When in season, game is well prepared here, especially the ptarmigan, a relative of the partridge.

Babettes Gjestehus
Rådhuspassasjen, Oslo
Tel. 22 416464
This recently opened restaurant, furnished with Norwegian antiques, is already a well-known spot. The chef's specialities include crustaceans, fish, and game. Guests are also offered a "Babette's Feast" menu, which inspired the name of the establishment, after the famed party described by the novelist Karen Blixen (Isak Dinesen) and later filmed by Gabriel Axel.

Bagatelle
Bygdøy Allée 3, Oslo
Tel. 22 446397
Awarded a star by the Michelin Guide, this exceptional restaurant is one of the best in Oslo, and offers Norwegian cuisine interpreted by a chef who has worked in France and has

revised his country's traditional methods of preparing ingredients and cooking.

Engebret's Café
Bankplassen 1, Oslo
Tel. 22 336694
Located in a small old two-storey house, this restaurant, which opened in 1857, is one of the city's oldest. It was once the meeting place for such famed personalities as the violinist Ole Bull and Henrik Ibsen. Its menu includes typically Norwegian dishes, especially delicious fish. In good weather, outdoor dining is possible.

Frognerseteren
Holmenkollen, Oslo
Tel. 22 140890
Viking style décor dating from the beginning of the century distinguishes this restaurant in the hills of Oslo, with a menu offering a serious choice of the best traditional recipes for meat and fish. Norwegians particularly appreciate the coffee here, which is served with tasty apple cakes.

Gamlestua
Kongensgate 23, Oslo
Tel. 22 416800
A little restaurant in a pretty antique format, all in wood, atop the large department store Steen & Strøm. Try tasting the delicious traditional dish *rømmegrøt*, a sort of porridge served with cinnamon and a glass of raspberry juice.

Gamle Rådhus
Nedre Slotts gt. 1, Oslo
Tel. 22 420107
Oslo's oldest restaurant, opened 350 years ago. Traditional dishes like cod, whose season begins in autumn, are served in this dark, old-fashioned interior. Try the poached cod and wash it down with red wine.

Be sure to reserve your table in advance.

Grand Café
Karl Johan's Gate. 31, Oslo
Tel. 22 429390
This café located in the Grand Hotel, is one of Oslo's most fashionable places. Munch engraved a portrait of Henrik Ibsen here. In 1928, Per Krohg, one of the masters of fresco painting in Norway, depicted the café and its illustrious clients such as Ibsen and Munch in a painting that was installed here several years later.

Holmenkollen Park Hotel
Kongeveien 26, Oslo
Tel. 22 146090
Located in the hills overlooking Oslo, the restaurant De Fem Stuer ("The Five Rooms") of this great hotel serves delicious Norwegian cooking in an amazing setting. The interior features traditional wood carvings, works by Gerhard Munthe and Theodor Kittelson, antique furniture, and wood-burning fireplaces. One of Norway's most successful young chefs won the Bocuse d'Or in Lyon in a competition against twenty-two international competitors.

Hos Thea
Gabels gt. 11, Oslo
Tel. 22 446874
A beige and blue interior is the setting for a menu served by this restaurant with only a few tables—which are often filled. The chef is one of the pioneers of Scandinavian nouvelle cuisine. His byword is quality cooking, whether of fish or reindeer meat, which he always prepares superbly.

Kastanjen
Bygdøy Allé 18, Oslo
Tel. 22 434467

This restaurant is called 'The Chestnut Tree' in Norwegian, because it is located in a street lined with chestnut trees. Traditional Norwegian dishes are served in this delightful setting at reasonable prices.

Lorry
Parkvn 12, Oslo
Tel. 22 696904
A simple, authentic restaurant that offers a choice of several dozen different beers.

D/S Louise
Stranden 3, Oslo
Tel. 22 830060
Decorated in the style of a transatlantic ocean liner, this sophisticated restaurant on the very lively port of Aker Brygge provides a fine view on Oslo bay. Norwegian specialities are served, especially fish. In good weather, Aker Brygge and its numerous outdoor cafés are the ideal spot for sipping a beer or tasting some shrimp while admiring the port.

Theatercafeen
Sortings gt. 24, Oslo
Tel. 22 333200
Decorated in the art nouveau style, this is the last surviving "Viennese-style café" in Northern Europe and one of Per Spook's favourite spots when he is in Oslo. A fashionable restaurant that is lively at any hour of the day. A must.

Værtshuset
Bærums Verk, Verkshusvn. 10, Oslo
Tel. 67 560608
The provincial atmosphere of this traditional little restaurant twenty minutes from the centre of Oslo is worth the trip: chickens and goats parade around the building. The dark-red

wooden house with rooms displaying lovely woodwork is the perfect setting for cooking that is much esteemed by the region's gourmets. The menus are mostly made up of delicious game dishes, prepared by traditional methods of cookery.

Jan's Mat & Vinhus
Breitorget, Stavanger
Tel. 4 524502
In a rustic cellar, a refined gastronomic menu emphasizes local ingredients, such as lamb from Rogaland.

Skagen
Skagenkaien, Stavanger
Tel. 4 526190
This former naval warehouse dating back to the 18th century offers a pleasant and unusual setting for meals based essentially on meat dishes.

Straen Fiskerestaurant
Strandkaien, Stavanger
Tel. 4 526230
This fish restaurant on the port comprises two rooms decorated in a charming old-fashioned style. The fish soup and burbot are excellent, as are the bread and pastries made on the premises.

Havfruen
Kjøpmanns gt. 7, Trondheim
Tel. 7 532626
"The Mermaid" is a fish restaurant set in a two-centuries-old former storehouse. The fish soup and creamed salmon are specialities of the house.

Tavern
Sverresborg, Trondheim
Tel. 7 520932
This large and splendid wooden house from 1739 is located inside the Museum of Traditional and Folk Arts,

the Trøndelag Folkemuseum. The tiny rooms decorated with antiques are very unusual, as well as the menu which offers smoked lamb or deliciously prepared reindeer meat. Bread and traditional desserts are made on the premises.

CAFÉS

Café Cappuccino
Kirkeristen, Basarhallene, Oslo
Tel. 22 333430
Located behind the cathedral in the shade of chestnut trees, this is one of the city's most charming cafés. It is only open in summer. Light meals.

Kafé Celsius
Rådhus gt. 19, Oslo
Tel. 22 424539
Located in a old stone building, in the oldest district of Oslo, this former 17th-century military hospital is a favourite gathering place for theater people and the press. In summer they fill the vast courtyard, and in winter they

occupy the large main room, where the atmosphere is relaxed.

Fridtjof
Fridtjof Nansens plass 7, Oslo
Tel. 22 335343
In this café located behind City Hall, businessmen meet for a drink after work to begin their evenings out.

Frognerparken Café
Vigelandsparken, Oslo
Tel. 22 443667
and Herregårdskroen
Frognerv. 67
Tel. 22 552089
In a majestic setting, the pleasant Vigeland park filled with statues, large trees, and a lake, these two cafés offer the passer-by a perfect stopping place for a drink in the middle of greenery, where you may contemplate the setting sun.

Kristiana Club
Kristian IV's gt. 12, Oslo
Tel. 22 428852
A large establishment which is open only in the evening,

including a café, a jazz club, and a discothèque in the Gustavian style, all interpreted in a Norwegian way.

Herbern Fjordkafé
Lille Herbern, Oslo
Tel. 22 149700
Facing Bygdøy, three minutes away by boat, this very pleasant café on a little island shaded by lilac trees offers light meals in summertime. A leisurely afternoon can be spent watching the ships pass by from the large terrace by the seaside.

Tre Brødre
Øvre Slotts gt. 14, Oslo
Tel. 22 423900
This pub with a warm atmosphere was opened on the former site of a glovemaker's shop. Today, a bar serving beer and wine is on the street level, in a lovely room with a turn-of-the-century ceiling painted with nymphs and cherubims.

Café Sting
Valberg gt. 3, Stavanger
Tel. 4 527520
This nice café perched on a hill that looks out over the port, hosts painting exhibits and also serves occasionally as a concert hall. In good weather, the lovely view may be admired from the terrace.

Dickens
Kjøpmannsgaten. 57, Trondheim
Tel. 7 515750

This café with rustic décor is housed in a former 18th-century warehouse with a lovely wooden façade. It is the place to go to taste the local beer, Lysholmen, in a warm and relaxed atmophere.

FOODS AND ALCOHOLIC BEVERAGES

Norwegian tables are filled with fish caught in their natural habitats, but also from aquaculture. Norway has the largest fish farms in the world. They produce trout, salmon trout, rainbow trout and many other fish which are exported the world over. Salmon is the king of Norwegian tables. Here are some addresses where a good choice of fish is offered:

Fish Market
Bryggen, Bergen
The fish market is one of the great attractions of Bergen. It enchanted the British travel writer Jan Morris, who especially appreciated Bergen in the summer. Every day except Sunday, a wide choice of fish is offered, notably delicious Norwegian smoked salmon, but also flowers, fruits, vegetables, craftwork and souvenirs.

Laks-Vildtcentralen A/S
Bernt Ankers gt. 8, Oslo
Tel. 22 111015
A large choice of fish can be found at this address where many of the city's restaurants go to stock up. Quality is assured.

O. Fjelberg
Bygdøy Allé 56, Oslo
Tel. 22 446041
This little neighbourhood shop in a charming street planted with chesnut trees attracts a rather chic clientèle. Besides a wide choice of fish (raw,

marinated and smoked), there is also reindeer and elk meat.

Aquavit
This brandy made from potatoes is very popular in Norway. Aquavit is to the Norwegians what whiskey is to the Scots. As with all alcoholic drinks in Norway, it can only be bought in state-owned outlets run by A/S Vinmonopolet, found in each city.
Norwegian aquavit, usually scented with caraway, can be clear, like the kind found in other Scandinavian countries, or amber-coloured. One of the latter types is *linie akevitt*, a Norwegian speciality. Whether manufactured by the Lysholm or Løiten companies, it undergoes a curious ageing process: poured into oaken casks that once contained sherry, it is loaded onto ships and goes off on a tour round the world, passing by Australia. The origins of this ancient tradition are uncertain, but the boat's movement, the sea air, and the varying temperatures certainly affect the alcohol's taste. It also acquires its colour during the trip. Each bottle's label notes the name of the boat on which it travelled. Lysholm is lighter and dryer, while Løiten is mellower and more complex. Both go extremely well with fish and red meats. Aquavit is generally served at the same time as beer, most often iced. Glasses of beer and aquavit alternate throughout the meal.

Chocolate
Sold in news-stands and grocery stores, Norwegian chocolate is much appreciated despite its modest wrapper. It is generally milk chocolate, as Norwegians are not very familiar with darker chocolates. Norwegians have

a sweet tooth, consuming an average of eight kilos of chocolate per person each year.
Two large groups share the internal market for chocolate. Freia, a large store inside the Grand Hotel, tel. 22 427466, has been one of Norway's most famous chocolate makers since 1898. This chocolate kept up explorer Roald Amundsen's morale during his Polar expedition. Tradition and renewal are the keys to Freia's success, adding up to the marketing of a range of 200 types of chocolate. Over the years, with its slogan "Freia, a little bit of Norway," this brand has become a real institution, supplying forty percent of the country's demand for chocolate and also playing an active role in the arts and culture. Since the firm was created, its headquarters have always been in Rodelokka, in Oslo. The firm's restaurant was decorated by Edvard Munch in 1922. In 1934 the paintings were transferred to the Freia Hall, a concert hall open to the public in spring and autumn for high-quality concerts. The factory site and the vast park which surround it are decorated with a remarkable collection of artwork, including sculptures by Henry Moore and Gustav Vigeland. (To visit, call for an invitation at tel. 22 381470). Another chocolate manufacturer, the Nidar Bergene Group, based in Trondheim since 1877, produces a great variety of chocolate bars. In Oslo, this firm owns a large store located in Brobekkveien (tel. 22 645110).

Beer
In Norway, beer is deeply intertwined with the cultural history of the country. The

first known brewery dates back to 1776. Made from high quality barley and very pure water from rivers and

glaciers, Norwegian beers are highly varied: red-coloured Juleøl is especially appreciated at Christmas, brown Bayer and Bokkøl beers are strong and highly malted. Pilsner, a lighter beer, is the most popular and perhaps the most refreshing, along with Brigg and Mackøl, the latter being brewed in the northernmost brewery in the world, at Tromsø. All these beers are sold in most grocery stores. The Ringnes brasserie financed Nansen's expedition to the North Pole. Some islands are even named after the brewery, such as Ringnesland.

CRAFTS

Blonder og Stas
Jacobsfjorden, Bryggen, Bergen
Tel. 5 318381

This charming boutique in an old wooden house sells linen, sheets, tablecloths and placemats, from every region of Norway and especially from Hardangerfjord, whose magnificent antique white-on-white embroideries are a particular favourite of the shop's customers.

Husfliden
Vågsalmenningen 3, Bergen
Tel. 5 317870
Møllergt 4, Oslo
Tel. 2 421075
Laugmanns gt. 7, Stavanger
Tel. 4 520703
Olav Tryggvasons gt. 18 Trondheim
Tel. 7 522762

The Norwegian Association for Crafts (Husfliden) has opened stores in several large cities in Norway, with Bergen's being perhaps the best of the chain in terms of selection and creativity. It is an ideal spot for buying a magnificent hand-knitted sweater. (The designer Per

Spook created a model for Husfliden.) Wool is also for sale along with guides for knitting sweaters by hand. Traditional crafts of the region, ceramics, glass and wooden objects, and jewelry and toys made of pewter and of bark are also offered. One-thousand years of tradition are juxtaposed with the best modern design.

Viking Design
Strandkaien 2, Bergen
Tel. 5 310520
The owner, a designer who studied at a fine arts school and who has worked for the country's most respected knitting industry, offers handsome sweaters with designs inspired by traditional older models from the 19th century in black, grey, and white or in the gentle tones of vegetable dyes.

David-Andersen
Karl Johans gt. 20, Oslo
Tel. 22 416955
This company which has belonged to the same family for four generations, has been making gold and silver jewelry since 1876. Their well-known stores offer the widest choice of modern jewelry or Viking designs. The same boutique can be found at Bergen.

Format
Vestbanen, Oslo
Tel. 22 837312
On two floors of a former railway station, this new boutique offers an interesting selection of contemporary Norwegian crafts: jewelry, ceramics by Ingrid Mortensen, glassware, sweaters and embroidery.

Heimen Husflid
Rosenkrantz gt. 8, Oslo
Tel. 22 414050
Apart from traditional craft products and the famous Norwegian sweaters, there is a rack of national dress, such as the *bunad*, still worn by Norwegians of every age on a number of special occasions.

Norway Design
Stortings gt. 28, Oslo
Tel. 22 831100
The loveliest models of glass, including those of Benny Motzfeld are available in this vast boutique which also offers a large choice of contemporary Scandinavian crafts: silver jewelry, ceramics, clothes and rugs.

Aune Keramikk
Kongensgt 27, Trondheim
Tel. 7 525382
Traditional ceramics from Trondelag.

ANTIQUES

Ellen Antikk
Vetrlidsalmenningen 8, Bergen
Tel. 5 328875
This charming boutique will delight all those interested in antiques, whether made in cities or in the countryside, in porcelain, silver, or glass. There is also a very fine collection of antique dolls.

Johan Albert Mohn
Domkirkegt 7-9, Bergen
Tel. 5 311373
This second-hand furniture dealer, well known among antique collectors in Bergen, offers principally Biedermeier furniture. Auctions are held six times a year.

Prydkunst Hjertholm
Olav Kyrresgt. 7, Bergen
Tel. 5 317027
Scandinavian decorative arts, ceramics, textiles, and antique glass.

B.A. 47
Bygdøy allé 47, Oslo
Tel. 22 442509
This little boutique located in the picturesque setting of Bygdøy allé offers a very fine choice of traditional wood furniture and small copper objects.

Gard Antikviteter
Schønings gt. 7, Oslo
Tel. 22 694483
Many small pieces of furniture, glassware, tapestries, and national costume are found in this famous antique shop.

Kaare Berntsen
Universitets gt. 12, Oslo
Tel. 22 203429
This great Oslo antique dealer is renowned for his large choice of furniture in city and country styles, but also for 18th-century glass from Nøstetangen, lighting fixtures, tables and antique country cupboards.

Loftet Antikviteter
President Harbitz gt. 25, Oslo
Tel. 22 444566
A large choice of furniture and country curios, painted furniture, glassware, etc.

Olav Skrindo
Industri gt. 60, Oslo
Tel. 22 606021
This antique dealer offers particularly fine country furniture (tables, cupboards, etc.) in lovely old colours, elegant bowls and textiles.

GALLERIES

Hordaland Kunstsentrum
Klosteret 17, Bergen
Tel. 5 900140
In a lovely 18th-century house run by the artists who show their work here—paintings, engravings, ceramics, textiles, glassware and jewelry are for sale.

Rekefabrikken Galleri
Nevlunghavn
Tel. 34 88783, or 34 88150
On the coast, to the south of Larvik, this former shrimp-packing plant has become a gallery for painting and graphic arts on a small island facing the port of the charming little village. The owner, Vigdisyran Dale, is a dynamic young woman who also owns a small hotel-restaurant in the same port, the Nevlunghavn Gjestegiveri, which is a charming informal spot.

Galeri Haaken
Lille Grogner allé 6, Oslo
Tel. 22 559197
Haaken A. Christensen, an art historian and noted collector who advises notables on their art purchases in Norway and abroad, directs this art gallery specializing in the work of Edvard Munch. Located in the residential Olso West-End area.

Kunstnerforbundet
Kjeld Stubs gt. 3, Oslo
Tel. 22 414029
This gallery of Norwegian contemporary art is an Oslo institution. Throughout the year it organizes shows and sales of paintings, sculpture, and engravings, but also of exceptional jewelry, notably that created by Tone Vigeland, and the ceramic work by Ingrid Mortensen.

BOOKS

Tanum Libris
Karl Johans gt. 43, Oslo
Tel. 22 411100
A vast bookstore where the able and often bilingual salespeople offer guidance among the wide choice of foreign books. There are

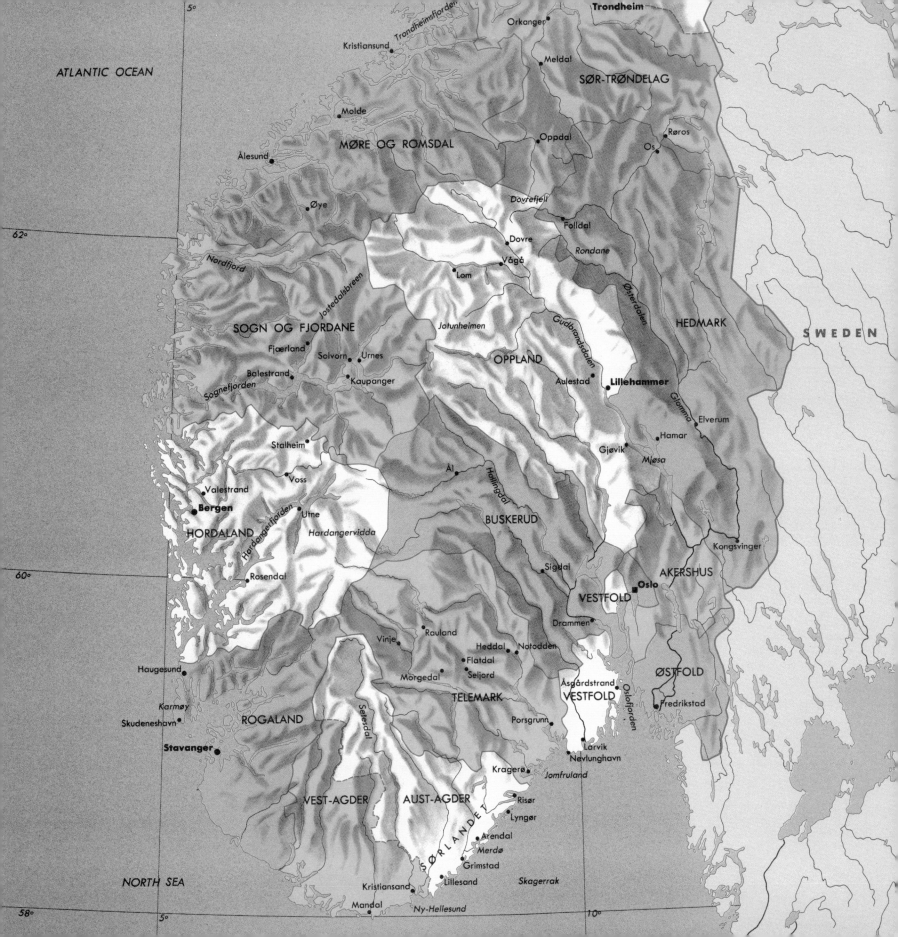

special sections devoted to Norwegian painting, architecture and crafts.

Erik Qvist, Bok-og-Papirhandel A/S
Drammens v. 16, Oslo
Tel. 22 445269
This modern bookshop, smaller than Tanum, places a strong emphasis on foreign literature. A wide choice and plenty of good advice.

MUSEUMS

Vestlandske Kunstindustrimuseum
Nordahl Bruns gt. 9, Bergen
Tel. 5 325108
A decorative arts museum particularly rich in faience, porcelain, and silverwork. The silversmiths of Bergen were famous for their large baroque designs. This museum displays some fine pieces from the 17th and 18th centuries.

Kunstindustrimuseet
St. Olavs gt. 1, Oslo
Tel. 22 203578
This decorative arts museum, founded in 1876 and recently renovated, is very pleasant to visit. The museum's masterpiece is the famed Baldishol tapestry, woven around the year 1250. Collections of textiles, clothing, jewelry and antique furniture as well as the most up-to-date Scandinavian designs are also displayed.

Nordenfjeldske Kunstindustrimuseum
Munke gt. 5, Trondheim
Tel. 7 521311
This decorative arts museum presents an interesting collection of Norwegian, French, and British furniture, as well as silver, porcelain, glassware and tapestries by Hannah Ryggen. The design

collection dates from the Renaissance to the 1950's.

Musical History Museum
Lade allé 60, Trondheim
Tel. 7 922411
Situated in the manor house of an old Norwegian family located at Ringve Gård (30 minutes from the city centre), this is one of the most appealing museums in the city. Musical instruments from all over the world are

presented in a lively way in each of the different rooms. The Biedermeier salon features one of Chopin's pianos. Music students give recitals on the instruments and informal talks on their history. There are also frequent concerts.

OPEN AIR MUSEUMS

Gamle Bergen
Elsesro, Sandviken, Bergen
Tel. 5 257850
Old Bergen is rebuilt here complete with painted wooden houses, boutiques and workshops grouped along the streets. The atmosphere of the town in the 18th and 19th centuries comes to life splendidly.

Vestlandske Setermuseum
Fana, Bergen
Tel. 5 915130
This open-air folklore museum is comprised of a number of typical houses from the western coast in the very lovely setting of

Fanafjell. A stroll amid these beautiful houses, which are still intact, really gives the impression of returning to the past.

Glomdalsmuseet
Elverum
Tel. 62 490407
This museum, the third largest open-air museum in Norway, gathers eighty-seven dwellings, chalets, *stabbur* and workshops which mainly originated in the eastern provinces of Osterdalen Valley and in Solor. The interiors provide exceptionally fine examples of painted furniture and elegantly decorated woodwork. A newer building houses a library containing 60,000 books on art and ancient history. At a short distance from here the superb Museum of the Norwegian Forest may also be visited.

Maihaugen
Maihaugveien 1, Lillehammer
Tel. 612 50135
This open-air museum, the largest in Norway after that of Bygdøy in Oslo, was created by Doctor Anders Sandvig (1862-1950). Fearing that the region's cultural heritage might be lost in massive waves of emigration, he began to collect old houses. A number of these still have their original furniture and accessories.

Norsk Folkemuseum
Museumsvn 10, Bygdøy, Oslo
Tel. 22 437020
A museum of Norwegian popular culture established in 1894, this is Norway's largest open-air museum (15 minutes from the centre of Oslo). A stroll through the vast wooded park threaded

with footpaths reveals 140 chalets and traditional wooden houses grouped around a fine 13th-century wooden church. Evoking the history and ways of life of all the regions of Norway, certain houses are richly furnished, and others are surrounded by gardens. There are also city houses, a 17th-century palace and Henrik Ibsen's library, rebuilt here while awaiting the opening of the Ibsen Museum in his Oslo apartment (currently in restoration). A restaurant with chimney and terrace tops off a pleasant visit in every season.

HOUSE MUSEUMS

Alvøen
16 km. west of Bergen
Tel. 5 325108
Built in 1797, Alvøen manor was the residence of the Fasmer family, owners of this former paper factory. Converted into a museum in 1983, the building, surrounded by a very fine park, currently contains a lovely collection of antique furniture, silverwork and porcelain.

Munch House
Åsgårdstrand
In 1897 Edvard Munch bought this little fisherman's house dating back to the 17th century. Purchased by the city authorities in 1944 and turned into a museum, its interior decoration has remained intact since the artist's death. In this "house of happiness," as the artist called it, Munch found the peaceful atmosphere and inspiration necessary for the creation of a good number of his masterpieces, notably *Three Girls on a Bridge*.

Bjørnstjerne Bjørnson House
Aulestad Farm
This writer, who, with Henrik Ibsen, created modern realist theater in Norway, received the Nobel Prize in 1903. Bjørnson was a great traveller, living in Paris, Rome and Copenhagen before buying this farm on the "Peer Gynt Road," where he lived until his death in 1910. The house, left as it was during Bjørnson's lifetime, is open to the public. The writer's office is particularly interesting, and features his handsome portrait by Lenbach.

Damsgård
Laksevåg, 3 km. west of Bergen
Tel. 5 343210
This manor, now open to the public, was built around 1770 and was considered at the time to be the finest residence in Bergen. It is a perfect example of roccoco wooden construction. The ravishing garden surrounding the property was recreated using the original plans, and only includes plants cultivated in 18th-century Bergen.

Hanseatisk Museum
Bryggen, Bergen
Tel. 5 314189
In one of the oldest and best preserved wooden houses on the Bryggen docks, this lively museum gives a good idea of what daily life in the home of a 16th-century Hanseatic merchant was like. Gathered under one roof are the merchant's dwelling and his offices. The apprentices' quarters with little box beds resemble prison cells, according to the French writer Julien Green, who called it a "concentration camp

universe," after being impressed by a visit here.

Grieg House
Hop, 8 km south of Bergen
Tel. 5 911791
Troldhaugen (Troll Hill), Edvard Grieg's house, built in 1885, is located in a magnificent setting on a hill overlooking a lake. The original furnishings, full of Victorian charm, have been preserved. They include a number of items from the collection of the composer, who lived here for twenty-two years. Next to the house, a concert hall that seats 200, offers concerts of chamber music at festival time. Grieg's chalet in the garden has remained as he left it at the time of his death. The musician and his wife Nina are buried in a little crypt overlooking the lake.

Folldal Bygdetun
Folldal
Tel. 624 90407
Uppigard Streitlien is a collection of high-quality houses and antique objects that was the vacation home of the noted Dr Anton Rabbe and his actress wife Tore Segelcke. Now a museum in which highly coloured interiors charm the visitor, it is a good starting point from which to discover the beauties of Rondane national park.

Henrik Ibsen House
Grimstad
Tel. 414 022
The Ibsenhuset, once a pharmacy, is the former workplace of the writer. The room where he began his literary career has been carefully reconstructed. It will be moved to Ibsen's apartment, which is currently being renovated in the city centre, facing the park of the Royal Palace. Ibsen's childhood home, Venstop, also may be visited in Skien in the Telemark region.

Det Gamle Handelssted
Kjerringøy
Tel. 81 21640
Situated north of Bodø, this former store, a symbol of the great North's prosperity, has become a museum made up of fine antique dwellings with carefully preserved interiors. The writer Knut Hamsun grew up on a farm in Hamarøy, now transformed into a museum, in the same Nordland region. Hamsun set his two-part novel *Benoni and Rosa* in Kjerringøy.

Ole Bull House
Lysekloster, Lysøen Island
Tel. 5 309077
This villa was built for the great violinist in 1872, about 30 kilometres outside Bergen. Its architecture is surprising, almost Moorish, topped by a minaret inspired by Saint Basil's Cathedral in Moscow. Inside, the rooms are decorated with a lacy woodwork that works its way up the walls. This summer home contained a concert hall, and therefore became a meeting place for the numerous friends of the musician and for personalities of the period's artistic and cultural life. The villa contains objects and furniture belonging to Ole Bull; its structure has remained the same since his death in 1880. The island itself, with its numerous footpaths etched through the property, a landmark site, is an unforgettable spot.

Merdøgård
Merdø, near Arendal
Tel. 85243
In 1736, on the little island of Mordø, a ship's captain bought a painted wooden house. Successive generations of naval officers and merchants have transformed the property from a simple house to the elegant dwelling we see today, with its refined 18th-century décor.

Oddentunet
Os, near Røros
Tel. 7 411165
At the end of the 18th century this ravishing family home, yellow outside and pink inside, belonged to rich copper mine owners in Røros. Inhabited until 1968, it was then transformed into a little museum of daily life in 19th-century Norway, keeping all its original charm. The rose paintings that cover the walls date from the 19th century and are signs of the owner's wealth.

Rosendal Manor
Rosendal
Tel. 5 481102
Located at the entrance of Hardangerfjord, this fine 17th-century manor features a baroque interior. This large stone building, situated in a region with mostly wooden constructions, was the home of a Danish baron who married one of Norway's richest heiresses. The park is famed for its rose garden, an idyllic setting for concerts during the Barony music festival in May, as well as summer concerts.

Bogstad Gård
Sørkedalsv. 826, Oslo
Tel. 22 504859
This large manor near a lake, 10 kilometres northwest of the city, is one of the finest estates in Norway. Built at the end of the 18th century, it is well preserved; its elegant salons and ballroom contain a fine collection of drawings and paintings, including a masterpiece by Guardi, all of which lend it a palatial atmosphere.

Vigeland-Museet
Nobels gt. 32, Oslo
Tel. 22 442306
Before the death of the sculptor Gustav Vigeland, the city of Oslo offered to transform his former studio into a museum. Now the studio contains drawings, models, woodcuts, and portraits of personalities of the artist's time. The museum is located at the south of Frogner park, where 193 large bronze and stone statues by Vigeland are displayed.

Emmanuel Vigeland Museum
Grimelunddsvn 8, Oslo
Tel. 22 149342
Sculptures, frescoes, stained glass and portraits are displayed in the house that Emanuel Vigeland, Gustav's brother, built to house his collection. The house is open to the public.

Stiftsgården
Munkegt. 23, Trondheim
Tel. 7 522473
This is the official residence of the Royal Family during visits to Trøndelag, and one of the largest wooden constructions in Northern Europe. Built between 1774 and 1780, the manor is furnished in rococo, Empire, and Biedermeier styles.

CRUISES

Fylkesbåtar
Dampskibsselskap A/S
Tromsø: Tel. 8 386088
Trondheim: 7 515120
In 1993, the Coastal Express celebrates its one-hundredth anniversary. Newer boats are added to the fleet of eleven constructions that visit 34 ports in Norway, moving from north to south and back, every day of the year. The boats pass by

Lofoten and the Northern Cape. A real Norwegian institution, the Coastal Express provides a leisurely trip, and offers you the pleasure of admiring landscape splendours from fjords to islands. A recommended crossing: an eleven-day voyage that goes round-trip from Bergen to Kirkenes. The ports passed during the night of the first crossing will be visited by day during the second part of the voyage.

HOUSE RENTALS

Tourist Office
Postboks 290 8301, Svolvaer
Tel. 8 871053
Most fisherman's houses on the Lofoten islands have become vacation homes. These *rorbu* were once inhabited during the fishing season from January to April. Now the houses have been restored and refurbished to make them more comfortable, while their original charm has been retained. Modern buildings have also been added, but in keeping with tradition. They permit numerous visitors to discover the charm of the little ports: grandiose nature, bird sanctuaries, and the pleasures of fishing in these islands.

Tourist Office
Karmøy
Tel. 4 827222
The houses and naval warehouses have been carefully preserved in this region once dominated by herring fisheries. Fishing cabins can be rented in Karnøy in a very good location by the sea. The Nornes house, an old boarding house, offers rooms and apartments in the centre of the old city of Skudeneshavn.

Kragerø Vekst
Torg gt. 1, Kragerø
Tel. 3 982388
Edvard Munch lived for several years in this seaside resort town on the southern coast. Here Munch painted *The Sun*, which depicts the gentle coastal landscape bathed in radiant light. The town is one of the best-known and most sought-after resorts in Norway. It is possible to rent a house through the local tourist office (the name of the office is Kragerø Vekst). Kragerø enjoys more sunlight hours than any other place in the country.

CALENDAR OF EVENTS

JANUARY
Tromsø: Aurora Borealis Festival. Classical and contemporary music.

FEBRUARY-MARCH
Cod fishing in the Lofoten Islands. Those looking for a remarkable experience can actually go along on a fishing expedition. However, modern equipment makes the fishing less spectacular to watch than in the old days.

MARCH
Oslo: Ski Festival in Holmenkollen.
Narvik: Winter Festival, dance, music, theater.
Lillehammer: Birkebeinerrennet, a historic ski race from behind Lillehammer to Rena (50 kilometres).

APRIL
Kautokeino and Karasjok: The Lapp Easter Festival. Traditional celebrations, marriages, baptisms and reindeer races.
Voss: Jazz festival, with performers invited from all over the world.

MAY
The 17th, a national holiday, also called "Constitution Day," since it is not a celebration of independence, but of the signing of the constitution on May 17, 1814. In every city there are large parades of children, many wearing traditional national costumes.
Bergen: International Music Festival.

JUNE
Bergen: antique boat regattas.
Honningsvag: Northern Cape Festival. Walk from Honningsvag to the Northern Cape (50 kilometres round-trip) under the Midnight Sun.
Saint John's Day: June 23, a holiday celebrated across Norway with fireworks and festivities.
Oslo: Summer opera; Mozart Festival, end of June, beginning of July.

Rosendal: Celebration of the Barony.

JULY
Risør: Grand Prix, small craft regatta.
Molde: International jazz festival.

AUGUST
Oslo: Henrik Ibsen Festival; theater, poetry, and music.
Risør: Wooden Boat Festival. The first weekend of August, wooden boats of all shapes and sizes gather in the port. Some are for sale. World Cup in ski jumping at Marikollen in the Akershus region, on one of the world's longest plastic springboards.

SEPTEMBER
Oslo: autumn festival (graphic arts, sculptures, contemporary painting) organized by the Oslo Artist's House and reserved for Norwegian artists.

DECEMBER
Oslo: December 10, the Nobel Peace Prize is awarded by the President of the Nobel Committee, which is made up of five members elected by the Norwegian Parliament (the Storting). The ceremony takes place in the grand hall of the University of Oslo, or as in recent years, at city hall.

SELECTED BIBLIOGRAPHY

GUIDES

Fodor's Norway (USA).

Visitor's Guide to Norway, Hunter Publishing Company (UK).

Norway: the Official Guide, Nordis Verlag (Germany).

Norway: Insight Guides, Harrrap, London (UK).

P. Bjaaland, *Living in Norway: a Practical Guide*, Bjaaland forl (Oslo).

Norway at Your Service, published by the Export Council of Norway (Oslo).

HISTORY

S. Mortensen and P. Vogt, editors, *One Hundred Norwegians: An Introduction to Norwegian Culture and Achievement*, illustrated with one hundred portraits, Norwegian Ministry of Foreign Affairs (Oslo).

A. Bryne, *Norway Behind the Scenery*, Cappelen (Oslo).

J. Adams, *The Doomed Expedition: the Norwegian Campaign of 1940*, Leo Cooper Publishers (UK).

F. Kersaudy, *Norway 1940*, Collins (UK).

J. Cornelius, *The Norwegian Americans*, Chelsea House (USA).

F. Nansen, *Norwegian North Polar Expedition, 1893-1896*, Greenwood Press, London (UK).

Norway Handbook, annual, Norskk Reisehändbök Publishers, (Oslo).
G. Opstad, *Norway*, Aschehoug (Oslo).

A. Most, *King Harald and Queen Sonja of Norway*, Aschehoug, (Oslo).

I. Libaek, *History of Norway: From the Ice Age to the Oil Age*, Grondahl, (Oslo).

J. Henriksen, *Norwegian Politics: A Primer for Non-Norwegians*, Aschehoug (Oslo).

LIFESTYLE, TOURISM

G. Jerman, *New Norway*, Norges Eksportrad (Oslo).

R. Spark, *Drive Around Norway: a Handy Guide for the Motorist*, Trafton Publishers (UK).

K. Habert, *Made in Norway: Norwegians as Others See Them*, Bekkestua (Oslo).

R. Asker, *Rose-Painting in Norway*, Dreyer Publishers (Oslo).

N. Ellingsgard, *Norwegian Rose-Painting*, Samlaget Publishers (Oslo).

J. Holan, *Norwegian Wood: A Tradition of Building*, Rizzoli (USA).

J. Stewart, *The Folk Arts of Norway*, Dover Publications (New York).

Arne Berkow, *Look at Norway!*, Gyldendal Norsk Forlag (Oslo).

M. Gilseth, *Fjord Magic: Getting Acquainted With Norway*, Askeladd Press (USA).

E. Welle-Strand, *Norway: Land of a Thousand Waterfalls*, Notrabooks, (Oslo).

K. Salvanes, *Salmon Aquaculture in Norway*, Institute of Fisheries Economics, (Bergen).

A. Riddervold, *Lutefisk, Rakefisk, and Herring in Norwegian Tradition*, Novus Publishers (Oslo).

ART

G. Bugge and C. Norberg-Schultz, *Early Wooden Architecture in Norway*, Norsk Arkitekturforlag (Oslo).

C. Norberg-Schultz, *The Functionalist Arne Korsmo*, Universitetsforlaget (Oslo).

One Hundred Years of Norwegian Painting, exhibition catalogue, Nasjonal Galleriet (Oslo).

Art of Norway, exhibition catalogue, Elvehjem Museum, Madison, Wisconsin, (USA).

K. Varnedoe and J.M. Stenersens, *Northern Light, Nordic Art at the Turn of the Century*, (Oslo).

Rooms with a View, Women's Art in Norway 1880-1990, exhibition catalogue published by the Royal Norwegian Ministry of Foreign Affairs (Oslo).

Neil Kent, *The Triumph of Light and Nature, Nordic Art 1740-1940*, Thames and Hudson (UK).

M. Nelson, *Norway in America: Four Exhibitions from Vesterheim*, (USA).

Ragna Thiis Stang, *Edvard Munch, the Man and the Artist*, Fraser (London).

Bente Torjusen, *Words and Images of Edvard Munch*, Thames and Hudson (UK).

A. Werner, *Graphic Works of Edvard Munch*, Dover Publications (New York).

Arne Eggum, *Munch and Photography*, Yale University Press (USA).

N. Grinde, *A History of Norwegian Music*, University of Nebraska Press (USA).

F. Benestad, *Edvard Grieg, the Man and the Artist*, Allan Sutton Publishing (UK).

T. Wikborg, *Gustav Vigeland—the Art and Sculpture Park*, Aschehoug (Oslo).

R. Frislid, *Cultural Landscapes of Norway: Man in Nature*, Landbruksforl, (Oslo).

LITERATURE

P. Johnson, *For Love of Norway*, University of Nebraska Press—Modern Scandinavian Literature in Translation. (USA)

Folk Tales of Norway, translated by P. S. Iversen, University of Chicago Press (USA).

P. Asbjornsen, *Norwegian Folk Tales*, Dreyer, (Oslo).

S. Sturlason, *From the Sagas of the Norse Kings*, Dreyers Forlag, (Oslo).

S. Sturlason, *Heimskringla or the Lives of the Norse Kings*, edited by E. Monsen, Heffer Publishers, Cambridge (UK).

P. Foote, *Aurvandilsta: Norse Studies*, (The Viking Collection, Studies in Northern Civilization), Odense University Press.

D. McDuff, *Contemporary Norwegian Prose Writers*, Norwegia University Press, (Oslo).

F.J. and L.L. Marker, *The Scandinavian Theatre: a Short History*, Blackwell Publishers, Oxford (UK)

D. Thomas, *Henrik Ibsen*, Macmillan Modern Dramatists, Macmillan Publishers, London (UK).

The Oxford Ibsen, 8 volumes, edited by J. MacFarlane, Oxford University Press (UK).

H. Koht, *The Life of Ibsen*, 2 volumes, Allen and Unwin, London (UK).

M. Meyer, *Ibsen*, Penguin Books, London (UK).

K. Faldbakken, *Adam's Diary*, P. Owen (UK).

K. Faldbakken, *Sleeping Prince*, P. Owen (UK).

K. Hamsun, *Hunger*, trans. from Norwegian by R. Bly, Duckworth (UK).

K. Hamsun, *Wayfarers*, trans. from Norwegian by J. McFarlane, Souvenir Press (UK).

T. Vesaas, *House in the Dark*, trans. from Norwegian by E. Rokkan, P. Owen (UK).

ACKNOWLEDGEMENTS

The authors wish to offer heartfelt thanks to all the homeowners who so graciously opened their doors to us and permitted us to photograph their universe.

Sølvi dos Santos particularly wants to thank Mr. Jon Braenne, Chief Curator of the National Heritage, for his valuable advice, the Norsk Folksmuseum for putting its treasures of popular art at my disposal, the designer Unn Søiland Dale who provided valuable help and enthusiasm, and finally, my family: my mother for her patient presence during this project, my daughter Camila, and my friends for their constant encouragement.

Elisabeth Holte would like to express her gratitude to her family who first introduced her to their country's beauty and refinement and has provided her with the means to enjoy them ever after, to Anne Fitamant-Peter who organized the exacting editorial work with professional skill, and to the documentation service of the *Aftenposten*, for its efficiency and research assistance.

Special thanks to those who gave valuable advice to this publication: Mr. Regis Boyer, Mr. Yan Meot, Mr. Frédéric Vitoux, Mr. Engström, as well as Richard Crevier, Céline Chesnet, Carole Narteau, and Stéphanie Houlvigue, for their help. Finally, thanks to Mrs. Tove Storsveen whose enthusiastic help has been an invaluable support in the co-publishing of this work.

The Norsk Hydro company, the most important industrial enterprise in Norway, sponsors important cultural events in Norway and abroad, (such as the recent Munch show at the National Gallery in London), tours of the Oslo Philharmonic Orchestra, and the creation of a collection of contemporary Norwegian painting. Norsk Hydro has helped in the publication of this book by making it possible for Sølvi Dos Santos to travel widely throughout the country to take the pictures for this book. The publisher wishes to join her in offering a hearty thanks to this notable company, founded in 1905, which is active in the diverse fields of petroleum, aluminium, chemical products and salmon farming.

HYDRO